STOP CRAVING HAPPINESS

STOP CRAVING HAPPINESS

Simple, powerful mind training for 10/10 happiness

IGGY TAN

Lofthouse One Pty Ltd

PRAISES FOR STOP CRAVING HAPPINESS

"Throughout my personal and business life, I have often drawn upon books I have learnt from, refer to, and often re-read – the Dale Carnegie ones in particular. I know this gem of a book will be another one"

Lyn Morten

"Where was this book when I was sailing the storm tossed seas of showbiz, with all its stress, competitiveness and pressure? By gee I reckon I would have won even more Logies and made even more gold albums."

Tony Barber OAM, TV Personality,
Winner of 3 Logie Awards

"Stop Craving Happiness is inspirational, truly inspirational. Well done on a brilliant book which I'm sure it will help many people in the years to come."

Peter Harold, B.AppSc (Chem), AFAICD,
Managing Director, Mining Industry.

"Stop Craving Happiness provides the reader with a great set of tools to lessen the impact of life's challenges, barriers and obstacles that often impact on mental health. A remarkably interesting read!"

Professor Gary Martin FAIM FACE,
CEO, Australian Institute of Management WA

"Iggy is a man on a mission. However, don't let Iggy convince you; let your experience convince you. This book can help you unlock the grips of cravings, worries, frustrations and fears... Take this for a test-drive."

Daryl Chow, MA, Ph.D. (Psych).

"There is so much more to this book that I'm finding makes a difference in life's journey. I am fascinated by its effectiveness and its potential"

Dr. Paul Sprague, MBBS, BSc, FRCR, FRACP, FRANZCR

"The most important thing that athletes must do to perform well in the cauldron of competition is to focus on the task and let the outcome look after itself. Clearly Iggy understands this need to 'live in the moment' and not obsess about (or fear) the outcome. This allows us to 'be' and 'do' rather than worry and fret."

Dr Ric Charlesworth (Cit WA, AO)
Australian Super Coach

THE COMMITMENT

This book requires you to be willing to commit just two minutes of your time to Happiness Sweeping® in the morning and again in the evening as regular daily practice.

If you are not interested in allowing four minutes of your time per day then there is not much point in reading this book.

Only with daily happiness sweeping practice will you improve and maintain your happiness.

The greatest things in life come with effort.

Are you committed?

© Lofthouse One 2018

All rights reserved. Without limiting the rights under copyright reserved, no part of this publication may be reproduced, stored or introduced into a retrieval system, or transmitted in any form or by any means (electronic, mechanical, photocopying, recording or otherwise) without the prior written permission of both the copyright owners and the publisher of this book. Happiness Sweeping® is a registered trade mark in Australia.

A catalogue record for this book is available from the National Library of Australia

ISBN: Paperback 9780994509512
       Hardcover 9780994509543
       Ebook 9780994509550

The names of the participants in the stories are altered to respect their privacy.

Published by
Lofthouse One Pty Ltd
Email: iggy.tan@bigpond.net.au

Lofthouse One Pty Ltd

Stop Craving Happiness
In collaboration with Jane Carew-Reid
Interior / cover layout: Pickawoowoo Publishing Group
Illustrations: Rachael Cassotti (Pictograph Pty Ltd)
Photos from iStock
Proceeds of the book will support Rotary International and
R U OK? (Suicide Prevention)

CONTENTS

Foreword xi

Preface xiii

Acknowledgments..xv

Introduction 1

Chapter 1   What is Happiness?..................................... 9

Chapter 2   Pursuit of Happiness 21

Chapter 3   Benefits of Being Happy......................... 37

Chapter 4   Secret to Happiness.................................. 49

Chapter 5   Happiness Sweeping® 67

Chapter 6   How Effective is Happiness Sweeping?.............. 87

Chapter 7   Why Does Happiness Sweeping Work?............. 97

Chapter 8   Taming the Ego Self............................ 113

Chapter 9   Meditation and Mindfulness.............................. 133

Chapter 10   Stop Craving Happiness 141

Final Dedication... 151

Author 153

FOREWORD

Dr Daryl Chow, MA, Ph.D. (Psychology)

As a practising psychologist I have great pleasure in providing the foreword commentary of this book.

Decades of research in my field has indicated that all approaches, when delivered by someone who wholeheartedly believes in their approach, and that the client resonates with, is equally as effective as the other. In other words, one treatment method is not going to work for everyone.

I am not interested in new methods or techniques. Today's literature on counselling, psychotherapy and self-help is inundated with hundreds of treatment approaches, each claiming to be more effective than the other.

Instead, my interest lies in first principles. What I mean by first principles is understanding the fundamental truths or origins. Aristotle calls this "the first basis from which a thing is known". For example, a modern songwriter might get distracted with the latest gadgets that develop fancier sounds for music. If they do not grasp the first principles in music composition from the start, the rhythm, bass, harmony, and melody, the songwriter is only chasing wind.

Iggy Tan proposes a practical method of "Happiness Sweeping" in his book, which I believe cultivates healing and change. I don't think there's a special "magic" in his approach as such, yet it touches on core healing principles and is hence likely to promote transformational change. At the level of first principles,

Iggy's approach holds similarities with other forms of medically-backed interventions in psychotherapy such as Coherence Therapy, Emotion-Focused Therapy (EFT), Eye-Movement Desensitisation and Reprocessing (EMDR).

When Iggy introduced me to his method, I was sceptical at first. While we spoke at a café he stepped me through his "sweeping" method (i.e. circular motion gesture with hands next to my head followed by the symbolic throwing away action); and it was awkward. Not only because I was trying this out with Iggy in a busy café, but it triggered memories of when I once attended a training session that was not based on core principles but a dogmatic new age method.

Thankfully, I persisted. What really intrigued me was how emotional I felt. My anxiety stirred around in my stomach and shoulders. I felt my eyes tearing because of the frustration and struggle I was experiencing at work as well as with my family.

Sometimes great innovation is developed from empirical science. But sometimes great innovation can develop from trial and error, and subsequently science catches up to provide validation after the fact. I believe Iggy's approach belongs to the latter.

Iggy has something credible to offer you in this book, but don't let him sweep you off your feet! Let your experience convince you. It is my deep belief that people can recover from psychological distress and even mental health conditions. Iggy's approach is one you can do on your own and I recommend giving it a go.

Dr Daryl Chow, MA, Ph.D. (Psych)
Psychologist. Henry Street Centre, WA.
Senior Associate & Trainer of the International Centre for Clinical Excellence (ICCE) Institute of Mental Health, Singapore.
For more on Daryl's books, articles and blogs, go to darylchow.com

PREFACE

The pursuit of happiness is a universal objective for every human being. We all want to be truly happy but the irony is that we constantly push happiness out of our reach. We delay our own happiness to the future by waiting for people, things and events to meet our expectation. Yet our expectations are rarely met which is part of the reason why true happiness is elusive. If we continue waiting, we will never reach the place of pure peace, contentment, joy and bliss.

Happiness is an internal state of mind and therefore has nothing to do with our external environment. The more you 'pursue' happiness, the less you'll likely find it. The key to happiness has always been in us; in our mind. In order for us to be 10/10 happy we need to tame the turbulence in our mind caused by the relentless mental chatter and suffering. Buddhist philosophy states that the existence of personal cravings and aversions in our minds creates mental turbulence. Consequently, by reducing the cravings and aversions we suffer less mentally and our overall happiness improves. While most of us would agree with the fundamentals of the concept, the challenge is how to achieve this in our modern and hectic, material world.

Happiness Sweeping®, a mind training technique that has helped many people dramatically improve their personal happiness and overall sense of well-being.

ACKNOWLEDGMENTS

This book would not have come to fruition without the generous assistance of others along the way.

Firstly, I would like to thank my wife, my soul mate and sceptic, Judy who recently joined me in celebrating our 30th wedding anniversary. To my children, Emma, Jayden, Georgia and Nathan who continue to provide 'wise owl' advice and are often the guinea pigs for some of the examples in this book.

To Leena Sheth, thank you for introducing me to Twin Hearts meditation, from which I have truly benefitted. You made this book possible through your commitment. Many and sincere thanks to Dean Tollis, my meditation teacher who is a fountain of knowledge and wisdom. Thank you for being such an excellent guide along our spiritual journey. I have learnt so much from our weekly meditation classes.

To Jane Carew-Reid, sincere thanks and appreciation for the editing and collaboration. The book would not have been possible without your work and understanding of the subject. To all those that have provided proof reading, advice and feedback; thank you for your kindness and generosity. Finally my sincere gratitude and appreciation to Dr Daryl Chow for taking the time out of his very busy schedule to pen the foreword of this book. Truly amazing.

To those that have already participated in Happiness Sweeping®, I am deeply grateful for your trust. I know that it was challenging at first and that the technique truly tested your 'comfort zone'. Your courage and perseverance has inspired me. Each of you has overcome what at first seemed like an insurmountable life-challenge. Your individual stories are humbling, but the happiness that you have been able to attain because you had the courage to attempt and then commit to Happiness Sweeping® has spurred me to write this book, with the view of helping many more people.

INTRODUCTION
OUR HAPPINESS JOURNEY BEGINS

BABY ON THE COVER

The first question that you may have already asked about this book is why put a baby's photograph on the front cover of what looks like a self-help book? To me a newborn baby symbolises pure happiness and contentment. Babies are born without expectation, cravings or aversions; the need for food and water is physiological. Babies are generally content, mostly peaceful (except when hungry, over tired or have a soiled nappy); they are generally in a blissful state of mind. A newborn's happiness has no reason; they are perfect examples of 10/10 happiness.

However, as a baby's mind develops from birth so too does its 'Ego self'. The Ego self is a sense of identity that develops over time and is formed from the vast array of experiences in life. The Ego self is defined by external factors such as social forces, experiences and relationships. See Chapter 8 for further definitions of the Ego self. Throughout this book I propose that the number one obstacle to allowing yourself to be truly happy is your Ego self. Adopting Happiness Sweeping® to tame the Ego self and nourish the 'Inner self' or soul is the key to attaining 10/10 happiness.

TITLE OF THE BOOK

The second question that you may have asked is why does this book have such a negative title – "Stop Craving Happiness"? The title sends a contradictory message especially for a self-help book. The book's title signals to potential readers to stop trying to crave happiness. Out of the hundreds and thousands of books and articles focused on attaining and pursuing happiness, this one tells us to stop trying. It doesn't make sense. All human beings aspire for happiness. Ask anyone what they wish for today and I am certain their first or second wish would be for happiness. So, the title of this book "Stop Craving Happiness" still doesn't make any sense. Well hopefully you will understand the reason for the title by the end of the book.

LET'S KEEP THINGS SIMPLE

In writing this book I have purposely designed it to be simple and easy to read. I have tried to avoid new age, spiritual or religious references. The concepts are kept general, easy to understand and thus hopefully sink deep and easily into the readers' mind. Basic ancient philosophies of happiness have been around for over 2,500 years and are the very essence of this book. Over the centuries however, mankind has tended to make these simple, ancient concepts far too complicated. We have re-interpreted and re-explained what were once simple teachings in an attempt to make them relevant to our ever-changing world. Unfortunately, in the process of doing so we've made the path to true happiness, enlightenment and self-actualisation far more complicated and confusing than it actually needs to be. The Ego self has played a big part in this. We have now reached a point where the modern-day person can no longer understand the very essence of the ancient philosophies that are the key to happiness. We have fundamentally lost our way.

THE COMMITMENT

As I mentioned at the beginning of the book, the journey to 10/10 happiness requires you to firstly be open and secondly, commit to the two-minute sweeping technique twice per day. Four minutes in total per day to nourish your Inner self is not a big imposition. The technique is a form of mindfulness, which helps you to become aware of your inner happiness. In order for it to be effective and sustainable it needs to become part of your daily life. The '21/90' rule of thumb refers to a theory that it takes 21 days to create a habit and 90 days for it to be part of your lifestyle.

By introducing this technique to people, the biggest challenge I face is ensuring the reader makes the practice a habit. During the face-to-face sessions, people feel better initially but when the session is over it is difficult to sustain the improvement without daily practice. One participant I previously coached, Ashley, benefitted from the initial happiness sweeping session with her happiness score rising from 4/10 to a fantastic 8/10. About six months later, I caught up with Ashley again and her score had fallen back to around 4/10; Ashley was bordering on depression. My immediate assumption was that she was not maintaining the sweeping technique, which Ashley later admitted, as she was busy and forgot. After a few more face-to-face coaching sessions she started regular sweeping again and her happiness score went up to 9/10.

Therefore, in writing this book I have had to ponder one potential downside, which is the lack of opportunity to follow up with you, the reader. Unlike the face-to-face happiness sessions, which creates a platform where I can keep in touch, remind and coach participants, it is unfortunately not possible to locally connect with every reader of this book. Therefore, this is why it is absolutely necessary for you to be your own happiness coach; you must remind yourself to practise the technique regularly. Only with sustained regular practice can you improve and maintain your happiness.

PEOPLE'S STORIES

At the end of each chapter you'll find a personal story from one of the participants, which recaps their experience with the happiness sweeping technique. The stories are raw and authentic accounts of the individual's challenges. More importantly, they tell of the improvement in their lives from practising happiness sweeping and they share personal tips of how they have modified the technique to suit their lifestyle. You will see that they have all learnt to practise pure acceptance, letting go and in the process detach their external environment from their internal happiness. They have all agreed to share their heartfelt stories in the hope that it could help someone cope with life's challenges better. I sincerely thank these people for sharing their journey and inspiring the readers of this book.

> "When people are determined they can overcome anything"
>
> Nelson Mandela

ANSWERS TO YOUR QUESTIONS

At the end of each chapter you will find a question and answer section where some of the most common questions I have been asked are included. I hope that the answers will help clarify the concepts in each chapter.

CONTINUE TO SEEK MEDICAL HELP

I encourage you, if you are feeling depressed or suffer from anxiety, to please seek conventional medical help including visiting your doctor, medication, counselling, meditation and any other medical therapy that is prescribed by your medical professional. Happiness sweeping is NOT an alternative to established medical or mental health treatment. Whilst it is very effective, it is only a complementary tool to improve overall mood and happiness.

MY JOURNEY TO 10/10 HAPPINESS

You are probably wondering why a business executive has written a book about happiness; a topic that belongs in the realms of self-help or new age. In this book, I describe my investigative journey with the exploration of how people can achieve a state of enlightenment or 10/10 happiness in our modern hectic world. Most of my friends would describe me as the most positive and motivated person they know. By nature, I am very calm, but a 'type A' personality. Family and friends would say that I would be the last person on the planet to suffer from depression. I am normally happy however, I have suffered depression on two occasions and to be honest I was perplexed when I was diagnosed. The best way to understand depression is that it is a condition or illness just like diabetes. Some people think that you can just "snap out of it". You don't tell someone with diabetes or cancer to snap out of it! What I can say is that when you are in the deep depths of the illness, your thinking patterns change and you cannot stop yourself thinking destructive thoughts. Fortunately, my depression was managed with effective treatment, medication, counselling and meditation.

Well, several years ago I started to become increasingly interested in spiritual development. So when Leena, a friend of mine, invited me to a Twin Hearts meditation group session, I was delighted to attend. Twin Hearts is a guided meditation that is practised worldwide and is based on compassion and loving kindness. During weekly meditation practice, my mind chatter slowed and a degree of mental peace developed, which is important in a hectic business world. Soon after, I was practising the Twin Hearts meditation every day. Meditation brought my mind peace, tranquillity and contentment. I would say during this time my happiness level increased to around 8/10 but not to a level of 10/10.

Coming from a predominantly scientific background, I was curious about the question of whether people were able to reach 10/10 happiness, despite the very hectic, highly material environment we live in. I wondered if it was even possible in the chaos of today's modern society. Isn't enlightenment only possible for monastic practitioners who choose to devote their life to spirituality? How can anyone be 10/10 happy with the pressures of work, mortgage, bills, raising children, marriage, health, relationships and so on? My curiosity to answer these questions led me to commence my investigative journey into happiness.

Valerie's Story...

I come from a large family of seven children of which I am the oldest; the youngest being 13 years my junior. I was raised predominately by my mother who my father left while she was pregnant with my youngest sibling. My mother raised all of us on her own both emotionally and financially. I always admired how strong my mother was and how loving she was towards all of her children even though she went without a lot because of us. She didn't have a car so everywhere we had to go, including the doctors' visits while she was pregnant, were all on public transport. My father hardly contributed financially to us and very rarely would he make an appearance to be with us.

I guess that I subconsciously assumed that all men were like my father and looking back on my life, I realise now that I chose men similar to him in my relationships. I now know that my father was a terrible narcissist and consequently my husband was also on the grand scale of narcissism. After four years of emotional, financial and physical abuse I have managed to come to terms with the fact that my marriage was not and never would be what I thought it was going to be. I married this man full of love and hope; that we would raise our families and take care of each other for the rest of our days. Unfortunately, after a short period of time he began to blame me for issues and circumstances that arose. I listened to him and was subjected to his manipulation. I blamed myself for a great deal of time for our marriage failing. When truths started to emerge, he became more violent and of course this followed with separation.

After four years of abuse I started to believe and blame myself for the marriage failure in many ways. What was even worse to deal with is that I felt responsible for subjecting my children who I love dearly, to the manipulation and abuse. After the separation, he cut my access to funds and I found myself trying to support my two teenage children with no way of paying my bills. I had to file an Apprehended Violence Order (AVO) with the police to protect myself from his violence. I was alone, sad and desperate. My happiness score was a distressed 1/10.

I learnt about sweeping after meeting Iggy some five months ago, through a very dear friend of mine. Iggy introduced me to the technique and I have been practising the sweeping method daily. I also practise forgiveness, acceptance and non-judgement. I truly believe this has gotten me through the darkest of hours and given me the strength to believe what is important in life; and to make myself a more understanding and an accepting human being.

Within a short period of time, my happiness level rose to a fantastic 8/10 and feeling very calm and peaceful despite the tremendous hardship in my life. This is some sort of miracle. I stay happy and peaceful even when my circumstances get worse. My friends have even commented on how forgiving I have been to my ex-husband.

Unfortunately I did lapse and failed to keep up with the regular sweeping and therefore suffered in a big way. I fell into a mini heap and was disillusioned and frightened. Iggy reminded me, out of the blue, about sweeping through a text message and I am happy to say that I am back to 8/10 again. I now feel so calm and peaceful even though I am going through one of the worst periods of my life. The result is that I don't worry or stress anymore and my mind is so clear. I recently found out that one of my rental properties will be foreclosed by the bank but the amazing thing was that I was so calm, peaceful and accepting. In spite of all my problems I am now living a life of peace and contentment. Thank you Iggy. I will never forget to make sweeping part of my life.

Chapter 1

WHAT IS HAPPINESS?

THE DEFINITION OF HAPPINESS

So let's begin our journey by exploring what 'happiness' means to people. Happiness is a fuzzy concept. People use the word all the time to mean many different things relating to the human condition. Throughout history, humans have strived to understand happiness and identify its sources. From around the nineties, modern science and psychology became infatuated with the study of happiness. There are hundreds and thousands of publications dedicated to the human pursuit of happiness, with specified methods contained inside every book, article and website for achieving that elusive state. This book is no different. Some of today's research centres conduct scientific research and experiments devoted solely to the concept of 'happiness'. Interestingly, there is also a field of study in psychology called 'positive psychology', which focuses exclusively on the study of happiness.

So what are some definitions of happiness? A number of sources link happiness to well-being or quality of life. Others define happiness as pure peace and contentment. Another argues that happiness is purely subjective, emotive and "relative to one's own experiences". On the other hand, terms like 'excitement', 'pleasure' and 'exuberance' have been used to define 'happiness'. Look up the Oxford Dictionary's definition of 'happiness' and it reveals a myriad of meanings and synonyms such as:

"contentment, pleasure, contentedness, satisfaction, cheerfulness, cheeriness, merriment, merriness, gaiety, joy, joyfulness, joyousness, joviality, jollity, jolliness, glee, blitheness, carefreeness, gladness, delight, good spirits, high spirits, light-heartedness, good cheer, well-being, enjoyment, felicity; exuberance, exhilaration, elation, ecstasy, delirium, jubilation, rapture, bliss, blissfulness, euphoria, beatitude"

OUR DEFINITION

Rather than trying to find a universal definition of what happiness means, which is rather an impossible task, I will define 'happiness' in the context of this book using four words: peace, contentment, joy and bliss. This definition of 'happiness' is more about a deeper internal state of being, commonly called inner happiness. Happiness is not the absence of any suffering, nor a lack of feeling a full range of emotions. Happiness is the ability to rebound from life's challenges, trauma and pain by returning to a state of peace and contentment quickly.

---

*Definition of 'happiness' is:
peace, contentment, joy and bliss*

OUTER AND INNER HAPPINESS

Research shows that people are no happier now than they were half a century ago, despite massive economic developments. The level of material comfort we all have today is equivalent to how the top 5 percent lived 50 years ago, yet people today are not much happier. Why is this so?

Dr Glen Mendoza, in his book *Better Person Mindset* describes two types of happiness: outer and inner happiness. Outer happiness depends on things outside ourselves like friends, environment, family, wealth, the size of our house and so on. Outer happiness also involves comparing ourselves to others in physical appearance, social acceptance or social status. According to Dr Mendoza, outer happiness is temporary and may not be sustained for a long period of time. Inner happiness, in contrast, is something that one finds within oneself. Inner happiness is always there irrespective of what may be lacking or what events may occur. Inner happiness is the feeling that you are sheltered and loved; it is living a healthy and balanced life; or experiencing a deep sense of joy in something that can only exist in the innermost reaches of your life. It requires regular training to develop awareness of one's thoughts, emotions and actions. This is achievable via inner reflection and meditation.

Along similar lines to Mendoza's theory, psychology professor Tim Kasser, who is known for his work on materialism and well-being, describes intrinsic and extrinsic goals as rewards relating to happiness. Extrinsic goals are focused on obtaining rewards associated with wealth or success; or rewards associated with one's image, looking good, having the right appearance, status and popularity in society. On the other hand, intrinsic goals are inherently satisfying in themselves and are associated with personal growth, close-connected relationships (with friends and/or loved ones) and a sense of belonging to a community (sense of wanting to help the world be a better place). Stemming from the Latin word for 'inward' intrinsic goals relate to the 'goods of the soul'; like personal growth, close relationships and physical health. There is a similarity between extrinsic or intrinsic happiness under Kasser's theory and Mendoza's outer or inner happiness.

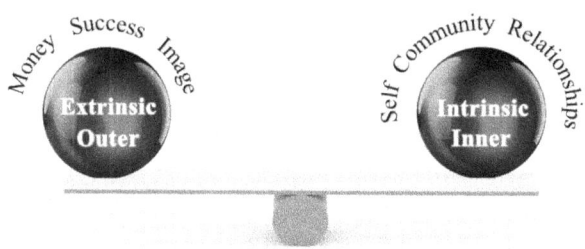

Based on decades of research Kasser identified that those individuals who were more concerned with wealth, status and image reported less satisfaction with their lives and therefore felt more depressed and anxious. Fundamentally, extrinsic goal-centred people described feeling less energised in their day-to-day lives. Conversely, Kasser's research has consistently shown that intrinsic goal-focused people were happier, had more vitality and suffered less depression and anxiety.

Positive, happy feelings are the result of intrinsic pursuits according to Randy P. Auerbach of the Harvard Medical School (McLean Hospital). "Intrinsically-motivated goals are thought to be inherently interesting, pleasurable and/or meaningful. Extrinsically-motivated goals are typically pursued in order to attain a reward (i.e. material goods or wealth) or to avoid punishment. Research has shown that pursuing both intrinsic and extrinsic goals can be beneficial, but not when one is at the expense of the other. Additionally, people who value extrinsic goals over intrinsic goals may neglect their interpersonal relationships and exert all of their time and energy in the pursuit of material objects and money."

A Daily Telegraph article (2017) reported that on average, men are most unhappy in their lives around the age of 45. They are an age group who have "lost their way" according to the research article. The Samaritans Suicide Statistics Report for 2014 shows that men aged between 40 to 44 are the demographic group with the highest rate of suicide, nearly four times that of women the same age. For those aged 45 to 54 years, the suicide rate is roughly three times higher for men than women. We (men) have generally spent most of our lives pursuing extrinsic goals like wealth, success and image in an attempt to gain ultimate happiness. During this journey some of us eventually realise that our extrinsic pursuits, driven by our Ego self, will never fully satisfy our happiness aspirations. We haven't been nourishing our Inner self along the way and this is fundamentally the problem. My belief is that women tend to do a better job at nourishing their Inner self and getting that balance right along the way.

In a 75 year-long study by Harvard University, which is the longest study ever undertaken in men's health and longevity, happiness was proven to be related to the number and quality of a person's relationships with family, friends and the community. In other words, the positive relationships we have keep us happier and healthier. The Harvard study explains that *"the social connections are really good for us, we are happier, physically healthier and live longer"*. The study concludes that the quality of our close relationships affects our long-term happiness. The researchers say that relationships are generally complicated; they take hard work and require a life time to nurture. But the most important point is that there are no quick fixes in relationships, you have to put in the effort and the work.

Ed Diener, a professor of psychology at the University of Illinois, was interviewed in a 2011 feature documentary entitled "Happy". Diener, or 'Mr Happiness', has spent over 30 years researching happiness. Some of his studies have found that a person's income is not necessarily correlated with happiness, whereas social relationships are correlated. In the documentary interview, Diener explains that we all need something bigger than ourselves to care about. His research has shown that the people that care for others besides themselves have a sense of wanting to help the world be a better place and a sense of belonging; they feel happier and more connected. In Chapter 8, I discuss the happiness benefits derived from the practice of 'less Ego, more others'. The practice of loving kindness and compassion to yourself and others is a very powerful way to improve your inner happiness.

WE ARE STILL MISSING THE POINT!

What is unfortunate about all of the aforementioned research is that it is allocating happiness to something external to one's state of mind. Even the intrinsic goals relate to community and relationships, which are outside of your inner mind. The biggest single mistake we make is imagining that changing the circumstances of our lives will make a big difference to our happiness.

We are missing the point and that's probably why happiness is so elusive and difficult to achieve or maintain. The intangible state of simply being happy is so hard to find. Even when we do have some happiness, it seems to fade faster than we'd expect.

The key to happiness has always been in front of us. Happiness is an internal state of mind. The more you 'pursue' happiness, the less you'll likely find it. Why? Happiness is simply your state of mind; a way of perceiving and approaching ourselves and the world in which we reside. Many people agree with the idea that happiness is purely internal and therefore has nothing to do with our external environment. Yet we attach happiness to people, relationships, image, success, material possessions and events that surround us. When these external things don't meet our expectations, we cannot help but suffer mentally.

The question is how do you reach this state of mind especially given the modern, hectic, highly material world we live in with all the stressful challenges? The answer is simple; you need peace in your mind in order to be happy. A brilliant quote from Indian spiritual leader Dada J.P. Vaswani on peace in your mind is, *"Happiness, true happiness, is an inner quality. It is a state of mind. If your mind is at peace, you are happy. If your mind is at peace, but you have nothing else, you can be happy. If you have everything the world can give - pleasure, possessions, power - but lack peace of mind, you can never be happy"*.

The key purpose of this book is to introduce you to the ways that you can bring peace to your mind. One way is a technique I invented, which helps you to detach the external from the internal state of mind. In fact, participants of the technique who practise it daily are still surprised how peaceful and content their lives are despite all the external traumas they face. Happiness sweeping will reduce your mental suffering and in the process improve your overall happiness and well-being.

"Happiness is not determined by what's happening around you, but rather what's happening inside you. Most people depend on others to gain happiness, but the truth is, it always comes from within".

Anonymous

10/10 HAPPINESS

Throughout the book I describe reaching the ultimate state of pure peace, contentment, joy and bliss as being 10/10 happy. So how do we describe this 10/10 state of pure happiness?

Participants who have reached this state describe themselves as being free of worry, stress and anxiety. These individuals will tell you that they no longer have cravings for wealth, success and material things in the same way they once did. In fact, they hardly have any cravings at all. Nothing makes them angry or frustrated anymore. They no longer fear getting sick, growing old or dying. They practise loving kindness and compassion to all those around them, as well as themselves. They no longer judge others and are extremely grateful for their life. They can honestly say they have achieved a cessation of mental suffering and are living a life of complete peace and contentment. They feel a sense of wonder, thankfulness and appreciation for life. Certainly, an enlightened state of being. Other terms in psychology that describe this 10/10 happy state are 'self-actualisation' or 'self-fulfilment'. From a Buddhist or spiritual idea, it may refer to an enlightened state whereby the individual's life is an awakened and compassionate one that is blissful and free of suffering. Yes, it is a bold claim, but it is possible from regular happiness sweeping.

Answers to your questions…

Q. How can someone who is poor be 10/10 happy?

A. Yes, of course, as happiness is an internal state of mind, you could be 10/10 happy if you are rich or poor, or in between. You cannot judge someone's internal state of mind from their external factors. That's why happiness is often indefinable as we are constantly looking for the secret in things, events and people around us. The secret of happiness has always been within us.

Q. Does an enjoyable external environment improve our happiness?

A. Yes, it can improve your happiness but it does not provide sustained happiness. We have been raised to allow our external environment to dictate our inner happiness. Eventually, we get to the point where our achievements, successes and external pleasures can no longer sustain our inner happiness and we then question the meaning of our purpose and existence. Eventually we have to focus on the Inner self and the state of mind where the secret of happiness sits.

Q. How is 10/10 happiness even possible in our world today?

A. The reference to the hectic and stressful modern world is an external factor and as happiness is an internal state mind, 10/10 happiness is possible. Of course, with stressful external challenges, typical of our modern world, it might appear difficult to achieve but through regular sweeping it is possible. As you will learn from reading the personal stories throughout the book, participants still face enormous personal challenges and stress. Yet all of them *have very high happiness scores and are mostly in a state of internal peace. As I mentioned before the Ego self is the major obstacle in allowing you to be happy. Happiness is a choice but we need to tame the Ego self to allow ourselves to make that choice.*

Lesley's Story...

I'm a 54 year-old woman who has a lot to be happy for. I am blessed with wonderful parents; great friends; two amazing children who adore me; a great job; a beautiful partner and a gorgeous home. Despite all of the above my divorce three years ago still makes me very sad and unhappy even though I have a new partner. I have taken medication, tried hypnotherapy, reiki and healing but to no avail. I heard about Iggy's happiness workshop and I decided I had little to lose. The fact it was free made me think it may be worth a go as Iggy was not into making money especially from us sad-souls.

I was very unhappy driving to the workshop with my happiness score well below 0/10 (yes, probably even a minus score if that is possible).

I took my sister with me. To my surprise I was summoned to the front of the session to be part of the sweeping demonstration with Iggy. I am in the medical field and I was a little sceptical at first but I am glad I attended the session. I was taking part in the sweeping technique, verbalising and throwing away various cravings and fears. At the end of the workshop, within 10 minutes, I felt a definite shift in my mood.

I became chatty with the group and my sister noticed me smiling. In fact all the way home in the car we both laughed and laughed. I felt a calmness, a pleasant feeling of 'all is okay' and my happiness score rose quickly to 5/10 within 10 minutes of sweeping. This was a great feeling and I actually asked Iggy if he hypnotised me.

Weeks later, if I had an issue that was upsetting me I began 'sweeping' and it does indeed lighten the burden. I don't know why, as long as it works I couldn't care less if it is psychological. I am currently happy and sitting at an overall happiness score of 6/10, which is a tremendous improvement from zero.

I sweep every day now and tell everyone in my organisation about that night of the workshop. I am not depressed anymore and for the first time in years, I am off medication. I was alive to see my eldest son's wedding last year and my youngest son's graduation this year. I am enjoying life like never before; my patients tell me I am glowing. My story tells it all.

Chapter 2

PURSUIT OF HAPPINESS

WHAT'S YOUR HAPPINESS RATING?

Throughout the book I make references to a 'happiness score'. So, what is a happiness score and what is the basis for this number? The happiness score is a simple question, "on a scale of 1 to 10, what number is your inner underlying happiness right now"? That simple. Yes, I am aware that self-rating happiness surveys are quite common, especially today, but a lot of the questions in these surveys refer to one's satisfaction with their external environment. For example, a survey developed by Oxford University requires participants to indicate how much they agree or disagree with a list of statements, such as "I am well satisfied about everything in my life" or "I don't think I look attractive". The statements are based on external factors like the participants' home, job, family, image, relationships and so on. Since our proposition is that happiness is only an internal state of mind, that's all we are interested in. How happy do you feel in your mind? Our external environment is irrelevant.

So, when commencing the sweeping sessions I usually ask the participants how happy they are (their underlying inner happiness) on a scale of 1 to 10, where one (1) is very unhappy and ten (10) is enlightened. When I ask this question to people it is amazing to see that most of them actually respond immediately with a specific number that has popped into their head. From my research with many participants, people seem to know exactly what their inner happiness score sits at. While it is only a number, a happiness rating will now mean something to you and no one else. The happiness score is used to measure a participant's progress so comparisons to other people are really not that important. Mr Happiness, or Professor Diener, uses a similar approach in his 'subjective well-being' index by asking a person how happy they are out of 10. Diener argues that in general people are the best judge of whether they are in fact happy or not.

So, how happy are you – the reader? There are no quantifiers to this scale, no survey, no statements, just your own personal score; an honest number out of ten that represents your underlying inner happiness.

Please record your score:

My score:

So, why is your happiness rating important? An area of process science, continuous improvement theory, believes that 'what you cannot measure you cannot improve'. In this way, having a happiness score is important as it helps you to be more mindful of your internal happiness state. By constantly monitoring your mood or happiness you are able to assess if the technique proposed in this book actually helps. Mindfulness of what affects your happiness is the first important step in this journey.

PEOPLE'S HAPPINESS

I am constantly surprised by the happiness scores I hear from both new and existing participants. People that appear to be happy on the outside might often report quite low scores. We are very good at hiding behind a protective outer face, which often prevents our true inner happiness from being revealed. We are embarrassed and sometimes shameful of our true happiness state. I am sure you know a person close to you that has suffered silently with depression and anxiety at first without your knowledge. That's why it is difficult to detect if someone is on the edge of suicide, as this outer face makes it hard to ascertain their internal suffering.

It is especially important that suicide prevention organisations such as R U OK? in Australia are helping people begin these conversations that could save a life. R U OK? is an organisation that is working tirelessly towards suicide prevention; having developed credible theories, their message is to highlight there's power in the simplest of questions, "Are you okay?".

According to this organisation, one of the most significant theories is by American academic psychologist, Dr Thomas Joiner. After his father took his own life Dr Joiner dedicated his academic research to exploring "why?" His theories address that complex question by describing three forces at play in someone at risk of suicide. The first force is that the person thinks they're a burden on others; the second is that they can withstand a higher degree of pain; and the third is that they don't feel connected to others. It's this lack of connection (or lack of belonging) that R U OK? wants to prevent. By inspiring people to take the time to ask "Are you ok?" and listen, we can help those people struggling with life to feel connected long before they even think about suicide. It all comes down to regular, face-to-face, meaningful conversations about life; asking "Are you ok?" is where this great organisation says we should start.

> "Happiness is the meaning and purpose of life, the whole aim and end of human existence"
>
> Aristotle

DO YOU WANT TO BE HAPPY?

Happiness is something that nearly everyone on the planet hopes for in some way or another. It is one of the only things we all commonly want in life and achieving it becomes our ultimate life goal. This 'pursuit of happiness' is even recorded as a fundamental right in the United States Declaration of Independence (1776). A famous phrase, "Life, Liberty and the pursuit of Happiness" has been interpreted as a right for citizens to live life in a way that makes one happy – as long as the law is not broken!

As children we are taught that happiness is especially important and pursuing it should be our fundamental lifetime aspiration. My parents would say to me "all we want is for you to be happy" or "we will be happy, when you are happy". As a society we are surrounded by constant cultural reinforcement that happiness is our number one shared goal, which is echoed through music, song, literature, art, media and so on. The United Nations adopted 'The International Day of Happiness' (also called 'Happiness Day') as a resolution in 2012 and the worldwide event has since been celebrated on the 20th of March every year. In its second year The International Day of Happiness was promoted by American singer Pharrell Williams with his hit song 'Happy', which is still the UK's most downloaded track of all time.

In the country of Bhutan, the Gross National Happiness (GNH) has become a developmental philosophy as well as an index, which is used to measure the nation's collective happiness. The concept was enshrined in the country's 2008 constitution, which declares that "the State shall strive to promote those conditions that will enable the pursuit of Gross National Happiness".

"We do not believe in Gross National Product. Gross National Happiness is more important"
                    King of Bhutan, Jigme Singye Wangchuck

Whatever we dream, hope or even do, there is always a deep, profound desire for well-being or happiness. Even in the fairy tale books we were read as children, the ultimate ending was that the main characters 'lived happily ever after'. Of course, most of us have been happy at some stage in our life but the challenge is maintaining this happiness. How can it be sustainable?

A few important questions:
1. Do you want to be happy?
2. Do you want your children to be happy?
3. Do you want your spouse or partner to be happy?
4. Do you want your family and friends to be happy?

If you are reading this book then the most likely answer would be a resounding "YES" to all four questions. Yes, of course you want to be happy. Yes, of course you want your children to be happy. We will come back to your dearest set of wishes at the end of the book.

The irony in life is that while we are constantly pursuing happiness, we keep delaying or pushing out our true happiness to another time in the future. Delaying is thinking we will be truly happy when we have a successful career; we will be truly happy when we are financially secure; we will be happy when our mortgage is paid off; …when the kids go to university; …when we lose weight; …when our spouse is happy; and on and on it goes. As we start to reach our happiness goals, we accumulate more and more desires and cravings along the way; we are therefore never truly satisfied. We keep pushing our own happiness into the future and we repeat this pattern until we die. We rarely get to a point in our lives where we are totally satisfied and content with life as it is.

Our loved ones or our children's happiness generally becomes a precondition for our own happiness and we suffer internally when they are unhappy. As you can see from the picture overleaf this is a very typical reinforcement of the kind of precondition I am referring to. As you probably realise, we fundamentally have no control of the happiness of the people we love or those around us. It is their internal state of mind. Yet we delay our happiness waiting for all our loved ones to be truly happy. That's part of the reason why 'true' happiness is so elusive.

Have you ever reflected on why people who are successful, intelligent and deep-thinking individuals fail to be 10/10 happy? We may have a loving partner and family, have many achievements and success in our job; yet, we are not fully contented and fulfilled. Part of the issue is that most of us are 'over-thinkers' who constantly analyse everything that is happening in our life, which is very draining and frustrating. The cause for our minds' turbulence and unhappiness is our high standards; we are too hard on ourselves and we're constantly searching for meaning in life.

It is admirable to have high standards though, right? Our Ego self has high standards for us. Part of the challenge in achieving true peace and contentment is that we know what we want and we don't settle for anything less, no matter what area of life we are talking about. This means that it's difficult for us to be satisfied with our achievements, relationships and literally everything that has a place in our lives. We tend to have idealistic views of the world. So when our expectation doesn't meet the raw reality of life, it inevitably leads to disappointment. Another reason why we fail to remain happy is that our Ego self tends to be too strict. We often analyse ourselves and our behaviour in a rigorous manner, seeking blame. We might recall a situation, which probably happened years ago, where we didn't act the way we should have at the time. We often experience (internally) these regretful flashbacks of our past mistakes. The Ego self remains unhappy with our past, which allows guilt, discontent and other negative emotions to poison our happiness.

Our Ego self will always dig for something deeper in our mind; a pattern, a meaning, a purpose. Our Ego self is endlessly searching for meaning. It never lets our mind and imagination relax and enjoy the simple 'good things' in life. We often crave for something fantastic, idealistic, or eternal; and, of course, we never find it in the real world. There is no point searching for meaning because there isn't one.

GETTING TO THE PEAK

Unfortunately we are 'programmed' from an early age to believe that the relentless pursuit of our goals will result in achieving success, a better life and thus happiness. This overarching idea is reinforced in today's mainstream film and literature where hard work, belief and motivation, i.e. 'never give up' are the keys to a successful, happy life. We climb the mountain so we can reach euphoric happiness when we get to the peak. We study hard for years so we can finally graduate. We work hard so one day we become a manager. We paint with perseverance so we can achieve a masterpiece. We are born with the belief that we can do anything – achieve greatness – as long as we don't give up. We compare ourselves with other successful people and we admire the fruits of their successes. The Ferrari, the mansion, the speedboat, the Lear jet and the holiday house in Monte Carlo; such things are the rewards for never giving up.

Unfortunately when we reach the mountain's peak, complete the masterpiece, score the ideal job, have the big wedding, or achieve the success we craved and strived for, this type of 'happiness' is short-lived. We believe that any suffering along the way is worth it once we achieve our goals, but unfortunately this doesn't lead to a sustained happy, fulfilled and healthy life. One happiness sweeping participant summed it up well by saying that it is almost an anti-climax. There is nothing wrong with goals but we need to learn how to enjoy the journey or the process, as much as reaching the final destination. This is learning how to be in the present or in the now.

Emma Seppälä, author of *The Happiness Track* says that our ideas about success that we teach our children are probably all wrong. She believes we are giving bad advice to our children about how to succeed in life. Most parents want their kids to be successful in life, so we teach them attitudes that we believe will help them achieve their goals. What we tell our kids is to focus on the future and "keep your eyes on the prize". According to Seppälä, instead of this we should teach our children not only to thrive in a chosen profession, but to stay true to themselves – and enjoy every moment of the process. Enjoying and being present along the journey is more important than the final outcome. This lesson will lead to inner contentment and happiness.

"ME" CENTRED UNIVERSE

I would like to share with you my simple interpretation of how we fit in the bigger scheme of things that might change your sense of self-importance. Today you are the person who believes that you are the centre of the universe; you are the person who can control the world; you make decisions that can change the course of your history and those around you. Anything you wish to do you can do, your mind believes that you are the most important being in the universe. Sometimes referred to as a 'me-centred universe'.

I will indulge you with an analogy. The human body contains approximately 37 trillion cells. Each cell type has a designated function and works synchronously with the other trillion of cells to carry out its function. Liver cells, blood cells, lung cells, gut cells, skin cells, brain cells, nerve cells and many more types of cells all working together as one unified co-ordinated organism. It is one of the wonders of the human body. Just imagine for a second that you weren't the centre of the universe and instead you were only a single cell in a body of 37 trillion cells. Yes, just a single cell. This time instead of your own body, the body is humanity (all humans living on Earth) consisting of some 7.4 billon people. Like a single cell in your body you have a specific function to perform in the humanity organism. You may be a carpenter cell in Brazil, teacher cell in USA, gardener cell in Australia, CEO cell in Thailand, dentist cell in Germany, mother cell in Indonesia and so on. You have a small but required part to play in the entire body of humanity, just like the cells in the body. As a cell you are part of one organism, which is humanity. Your individual function and purpose as a cell adds to the overall organisation and function of humanity – and that's it.

When it is time, as a single cell (who once thought it was the centre of the organism) you will eventually die. You will cease to exist and another cell will replace you; but nothing will stop the whole humanity organism from living. As a cell in the body of humanity you are not necessarily vital, however, you are part and one with the humanity body. So stop taking everything so seriously as you are just a single cell after all. Stop worrying about the future, you are just a single cell. Stop looking for meaning, there is no meaning for cells. There is no right or wrong and there is no good or bad. It is what it is. You exist only to perform a function, so do it well and with passion. Some cells die early, some cells get sick. Some cells kill other cells. Give up the idea that you are the centre of the universe. If you start to think that you, as a single cell, can control the body consisting of 37 trillion cells then you will never live a satisfied or fulfilled life. Perform your function and purpose as a cell well. Treat other cells with kindness and compassion as they are a part of you. Enjoy being present and be happy as a single cell. Let go!

Ultimately, we aren't as important as we think we are. So am I trying to depress you, you may ask? No, I am just trying to tame your

Ego self and help you let go of trying to change everything around you and let go of the idea that you have any control of everything you believe you can control. This ultimate acceptance and letting go is the final part of achieving 10/10 happiness.

Throughout the book I quote His Holiness the Dalai Lama; I am a big fan of his wisdom. He speaks simply and straight to the heart. As an example of our significance in the universe, His Holiness famously said, *"Given the scale of life in the cosmos, one human life is no more than a tiny blip. Each one of us is just a visitor to this planet, a guest, who will only stay for a limited time. What greater folly could there be than to spend this short time alone, unhappy or in conflict with our companions? Far better, surely, to use our short time here in living a meaningful life, enriched by our sense of connection with others and being of service to them"*.

Answers to your questions…

Q. Do I need to change my life strategies for achieving happiness?

A. I was speaking to a friend who had been very successful at achieving his constant goals over many decades – his life strategy. His job was high paying, he had wealthy assets, a loving wife and family; and I asked him how did this strategy help him with inner happiness? He admitted it didn't; he was unhappy with a score of 4/10, angry and suffering from depression. Suffering to get to the peak does not make us any happier. We need to nourish our Inner self (soul) along the way and learn to be in the present.

Q. Doesn't achievement of goals make you happier?

A. As children we are raised to believe that extrinsic goals and objectives are the source of motivation and achievement. When we achieve these goals, we feel elated and happy (like a sugar hit). Unfortunately, this elated feeling doesn't last long and we start the process of chasing more external goals again. A friend of mine, who climbed a mountain in Tibet, gave a great example. He said that most of the climbers on the expedition up the mountain struggled for a week to scale the mountain and when they reached the peak, they felt elated and on top of the world. Then they struggled for another week to get down the mountain. Happiness from achieving a goal is short-lived and temporary. On the other hand, this friend (10/10) admitted he simply enjoyed the climb, the scenery, the people, the Tibetan culture and spirituality. The descent was exactly the same. He was present amongst the scenery, nature, tranquillity and spirituality of the mountain. Other climbers were focused on reaching the peak; they missed the happiness of the journey.

Ashley's Story...

I'm a 44 year-old woman with an original happiness score of between 2-3/10 and some days a 0/10. For as long as I can remember I have always been a little extreme. Quite often I liked to escape, shut the world out and recharge. I think I was happiest when I first lived on my own and could easily just unplug the phone, not answer the door and chill. I either like to party and be very social or be at home alone. A few challenges with relationships during the early years, my confidence and self-worth dropped; until I started to mature and realise it reflected on them and not me.

Next, marriage and kids. An unplanned pregnancy at a time when I was still wanting to take on the world, travel and finish university. I wasn't at my happiest. A very difficult birth and nearly losing the baby who ended up being very challenging and in hindsight, I suffered post-natal depression.

That baby (soon to be an adult) has never been easy. Full of energy (ADHD) and never sleeping or even slowing down, a very high IQ (154 - Mensa) and an inability to self regulate his temper. Parenting him has never been easy. It used to really exhaust and depress me that parenting and life was difficult and didn't look like my ideal dream. I could never live up to my expectation of a working mum; a sports mum; a school mum; a great wife; a great daughter; a great sister and the queen of hosting with lots of friends.

I always felt anger, I was frustrated and I felt alone. My husband worked nights and weekends (still does) and even though it was great that he could have our son during the day I was left to 'deal' with him on my own at a time when he was always at his most difficult. Throw in the mix a rare genetic disorder and him being sick every six weeks;

I have to admit I was nearly done for.

Fast forward a few years: a marriage with the usual challenges; a career change; a second child; possibly not the greatest idea but I was determined to have a daughter. I had my baby girl and we spent the best part of a year in and out of hospital with her having a serious lung condition and what was later diagnosed as another rare (non-related) genetic disorder.

So, now I have two children with rare disorders and the overwhelming feeling of guilt and grief that suffocates you. With the kids being seven and a half years apart in age, one with a crazy IQ and one with a borderline IQ. I quickly realised I had a long battle ahead and I wasn't sure I was capable of the challenge.

I have known Iggy for a while and when out one night with friends, I quite possibly may of had too much to drink (my preferred crutch and escape) I started talking to Iggy and he talked to me about happiness sweeping. He told me to give him a call. I must have been low at the time because I am the queen of a good masked face. I never like to show that I don't have it all under control. Somehow though, I made the call, put my pride and my expectations in the glovebox and caught up for a chat.

My initial thought "I need what Iggy is on". No, seriously, at first I was really embarrassed, I didn't like sharing what I saw as my failings and how weak and vulnerable I was. Then as Iggy talked, I relaxed and thought well if I am going to do it, I'll embrace it and be truthful and honest. Iggy has that way of enabling you to want to tell him stuff that you normally wouldn't. He introduced me to happiness sweeping and I began to use it daily. The sweeping practice was a bit left field but I had been exposed to some similar thinking as my husband is a little left and alternative. The technique was something that was achievable; it didn't involve me taking time out of a hectic schedule. It was easy enough to remember and implement.

The initial results of the sweeping were really good; even the kids would comment; my stress and anxiety came down considerably. My self-belief was also up. Initially, there were challenges trying to practise the sweeping due to consistency, messy thoughts and loud noises in my head, it was like everything was spewing out, all at once. I now make the sweeping a regular habit by adapting it. I am a lover of showers, so while showering each morning, I identify and wash away each craving and aversion. I visualise them all running out of my body down the drain and then white light running through making it all clear and bright. I also initially wrote on mirrors and post-it notes stuck onto the kitchen cupboards to remind me to sweep.

My advice to others, whilst it sounds a little cliché, is that "nothing is easy that is worthwhile". You have nothing to lose and yet you will have so much to gain by trying Iggy's sweeping technique. Once formed, the technique is individualised and habitual; it's easy; quick; transportable and can be used anywhere and at any time. What a gift to yourself and to the ones that love you.

The personal benefit of the sweeping technique and coaching is immense. I can self-monitor now, I don't get it right all the time but mostly I can get to a stage where I don't implode anymore. For example, I use the sweeping technique before meetings, be it at work, school, business or at home; I go through the process and talk myself down from the ledge by using it. My happiness score now is generally close to 10/10 even during tough weeks. I no longer drink. My son is most of the time brilliant now and I really enjoy hanging out with him. I am generally contented, peaceful and calm. This is a miracle for me!

Chapter 3

BENEFITS OF BEING HAPPY

HAPPY HEALTH

Happiness and good health go hand-in-hand. From my personal experience, when I commenced regular happiness sweeping my happiness improved. My physical health and well-being also improved to the point where I now rarely get sick. I may pick up a few sniffles or a slight cold from travelling but recover quickly. My blood pressure is the best it has ever been and I generally feel and look younger. Scientific studies have found that happiness can make our hearts healthier, our immune systems stronger and our lives longer.

HAPPINESS PROTECTS YOUR HEART

Kira Newman, a journalist for the Greater Good Science Centre at UC Berkeley, has written articles on the topic of the health benefits from being happy. According to Newman, many scientific studies conducted over the past decade show the correlation between happiness and a healthier cardiovascular system. In a 2005 paper, it was found that happiness is a predictor for lower heart rate and blood pressure. The 'happiest' participants in the study displayed an average of six beats per minute lower for heart rate and better blood pressure. A similar study undertaken in 2010 involving 2,000 Canadians attempted to test the link between happiness levels and coronary heart disease. The study concluded that the participants with higher levels of mental well-being were less likely to have developed coronary heart disease. In fact, for each one-point increase in happiness they had expressed, their heart disease risk was 22 percent lower.

HAPPINESS STRENGTHENS OUR IMMUNE SYSTEMS

Research has also found a link between happiness and a stronger immune system. In Newman's article (2015) she suggests that we probably know of an unhappy and/or angry person who always seems to be getting sick. This may be no coincidence according to Newman; researchers in the United States investigated why 'happier' people might be less susceptible to sickness. In 2006 the researchers gave 81 graduate students the hepatitis B vaccine. The results showed that the 'happiest' participants were nearly twice as likely to have a high antibody response to the vaccine, which is a sign of a robust immune system. Instead of merely minimising the symptoms, happiness seemed to be literally working at a cellular level.

HAPPINESS COMBATS STRESS

According to Newman, stress triggers biological changes to our hormones and blood pressure. Happiness seems to help us recover from stress quickly. Interestingly, in the Hep-B study of 2006, the happiest participants had 23 percent lower levels of the stress hormone, cortisol. In addition, the level of a blood-clotting protein that increases after stress was 12 times lower. This study concludes that happiness also seems to carry benefits even when stress is inevitable.

HAPPY PEOPLE HAVE FEWER ACHES AND PAINS

Unhappiness can be painful – literally. A 2001 study investigated the link between positive emotions and pain management. In this study, participants were asked to rate their most recent experience of a positive emotion, then (five weeks later) they were asked how much they had experienced negative symptoms like muscle strain, dizziness and heartburn since the study began. The study concluded that people who reported the highest levels of positive emotion at the beginning actually became healthier over the course of the study and ended up healthier than their unhappy counterparts.

"Calm mind brings inner strength and self-confidence, so that's very important for good health"

Dalai Lama

HAPPINESS COMBATS DISEASE AND DISABILITY

Happiness has been found to be associated with improvements in more severe, long-term conditions as well, not just shorter-term aches and pains. A 2008 study of nearly 10,000 Australians examined the link between happiness and the participants' abilities to combat long-term disease. The extensive research concluded that participants who reported being happy and satisfied with life most or all of the time were about 1.5 times less likely to have long-term health conditions (chronic pain and serious vision disorders) two years later.

HAPPINESS LENGTHENS OUR LIFESPANS

In the end the ultimate health indicator is longevity. In perhaps the most well-known study in happiness and longevity (1986 National

Institute on Ageing) a total of 678 American Roman Catholic sisters who were members of the School Sisters of Notre Dame participated in the study. The nuns were used in the study because they represent a relatively homogeneous group (no drug use, little or no alcohol, similar housing and reproductive histories, etc.), which minimised the extraneous variables. The study concluded that the life expectancy of the group of Catholic nuns was linked to the amount of positive emotion they expressed in an autobiographical essay they wrote upon entering the convent decades earlier. Typically the essays were written while the nuns were in their 20s. The results of the study found the 'happier' nuns lived approximately 7-10 years longer than the least happy.

Similarly, a study (2011) in the UK asked almost 4,000 British adults aged between 52 and 79 how happy, excited and content they were multiple times in a single day. Here, happier people were 35 percent less likely to die over the course of about five years than their unhappier counterparts.

HAPPINESS IMPROVES PRODUCTIVITY

You know yourself that when you are happy, free from worry and stress, your productivity and creativity can 'go through the roof'. Positive thoughts result in positive actions and in turn, enhance your productivity. No wonder happy students are generally luckier in exams and happy workers are generally more successful. From your experience you probably agree that a calm, worry-free person is more productive in the workplace.

Jennifer Moss from Plasticity Consulting Group claims that happy, high-performing workplace cultures earn as much as 50 percent more revenue and have the highest levels of both employee and customer satisfaction. The Harvard Business Review undertook an analysis of hundreds of studies showing an average of 31 percent higher productivity, 37 percent higher sales, with creativity three times higher from happier workplace cultures.

HAPPINESS AND CREATIVITY

So is there a link between happiness and creativity? Back in 1996 Psychology Today published an article by Robert Epstein, attesting that "greater creativity breeds greater happiness". The creative process is itself a source of joy for most people. Epstein stated that happy people are more creative because, in general, they have the mental capacity, grit and willingness to explore, which are all critical factors for harnessing creativity. More recent scientific research suggests creative output increases with happiness. According to psychologist Adam Anderson, co-author of a University of Toronto study linking the two, *"with positive mood, you actually get more access to things you would normally ignore. Instead of looking through a porthole, you have a landscape or panoramic view of the world."* Creativity researcher Dr Shelley Carson observed from her studies that *"increases in positive mood broadens attention and allows us to see more possible solutions to solve creative problems."*

Professor Teresa Amabile, a Harvard researcher in individual productivity, team creativity and organisational innovation was interested in examining the same link between happiness and creativity. In her study she asked 280 people employed in various industries to record their daily emotions. She studied 12,000 journal entries and concluded that creativity is positively associated with joy and love and negatively associated with anger, fear and anxiety.

DEPRESSION AND ANXIETY

Of course the other end of the health spectrum is depression and anxiety. Depression is a modern health epidemic in developed countries and is the single-most challenging and damaging health issue of today. In fact, one million Australians suffer from depression in any one year and over two million suffer from anxiety. We lose about eight people per day to suicide in Australia. Almost half the people reading this book will suffer from a mental illness in their lifetime.

Our employees' mental health in the workplace is also of concern. Today we are seeing more and more absenteeism, presenteeism (working longer hours) and compensation claims due to mental health conditions. Untreated depression results in over six million working days lost each year in Australia. According to a PWC report on mental health in the workplace, the impact of mental health conditions is estimated to be worth approximately $10.9 billion per year. In Australia, $4.7 billion of this is in absenteeism, $6.1 billion in presenteeism and $145.9 million in compensation claims.

One traditional hypothesis of depression is that people who are depressed have low levels of neurotransmitters like serotonin in the brain. But growing evidence supports that at least some forms of depression may also be linked to ongoing low-grade inflammation in the body. A new study published in The Journal of Clinical Psychiatry supports the premise that increased inflammation may play a role in depression. The study examined data from over 14,000 people who had blood samples taken and were interviewed between 2007 and 2012. They found that people with depression had 46 percent higher levels of C-reactive protein, a marker of inflammatory disease, in their blood samples. The study was able to establish an association between depression and inflammation.

Chronic stress has been shown to worsen inflammation in the brain, leading to both harmful physical and mental effects. As human beings, we are built with the inherent 'fight or flight' response. However, in today's society we still face the same intense stress stimuli similar to a dangerous sabretooth tiger as our predecessors, but we cannot run or fight, which would serve to relieve stress hormones. Instead this stress builds up, which is one of the reasons behind the theory of brain inflammation causing depression. So reducing stress to the brain, through meditation, mindfulness, calm breathing or happiness sweeping, will likely reduce inflammation and bring peace, contentment and clarity in your mind.

Answers to your questions…

Q. Do you recommend medication if suffering from depression?

A. Yes, absolutely, if prescribed by your doctor. As mentioned at the front of this book, I encourage you, if you are feeling depressed or suffer from anxiety, to seek conventional medical help. Happiness sweeping is not an alternative to established medical or mental health treatment. Happiness sweeping has never been clinically tested for the treatment of depression. Whilst it is very effective, it is only a complimentary tool to improve overall mood and happiness. If you use happiness sweeping and it makes you feel happy then keep using it.

Q. How can we be happy if we are experiencing hardship?

A. When you wait for periods of your life when there are no hardships then your happiness will be sporadic. If you want to be happy all the time then you need to learn to detach from the external environment affecting your internal happiness. This might seem impossible but the regular practice of happiness sweeping has been found to be effective at doing so. As in the participant's stories, people like John (Chapter 9) who is suffering from Multiple Sclerosis; has a partner with psychological problems; going through a separation; and having financial issues. John now maintains an amazing happiness score of 10 and you can't miss his smile, it is infectious. You may ask, what sort of drugs is he taking? Through his regular happiness sweeping and meditation, he practices pure acceptance of his life's hardships and in the process he is able to detach the external worries from his internal state of happiness. He often says that it is unbelievable how he can be so happy under the circumstances. John's story, like many of the other participants' in this book, is truly inspirational.

Alfred's Story...

I am 62 years-old. Before being introduced to happiness sweeping, I sat with a very low happiness score of 4/10. I come from a sporting/AFL background where motivation is a key to peak performance and winning results. I played AFL for over 12 years and achieved over 200 games. There were a number of personal achievements but we did not make the Holy Grail, the AFL premiership. This always ate away within me but I realised that my journey was a good one; so be satisfied with what I had achieved. I coached for a few years and had success winning two premierships; and guided a few young men into AFL careers.

I married in 1984 to my childhood sweetheart. Due to difficulty having children we enrolled in the IVF program, however after 10 unsuccessful attempts and a number of years later we decided to adopt. We adopted a beautiful baby boy of 7 weeks-old from Sri Lanka. One year later, another son came along by the virtue of being a frozen embryo through the IFV program. He was in a rush to enter the world arriving at 23 weeks gestation and weighing at a tiny 500 grams. It was not an easy first few weeks and months but he is now 23 and a strapping young photographer travelling the world.

Whilst playing AFL, I ran my own manufacturing business employing 20 people; which lasted 25 years until cheap Chinese imports started to destroy Australian manufacturing. This eventually broke the business and with that we lost our home and livelihood. It was devastating; we had to start all over again at the age of 50! There were no jobs and the future looked very bleak for us. But with help from good friends we pushed on. I started working in men's fashion, which led me to where I am today; advertising/sales in publishing within the mining industry. My wife worked as a receptionist for

3 years. She then joined Virgin Airlines as a flight attendant and she is still there, loving her job in training.

Losing everything materially was heartbreaking but nothing compared to what was coming. My adopted eldest son had a mental breakdown and tried to kill himself a couple of times. We sent him to the doctors to work through these mental issues. Tragically, he took the life of his girlfriend after suffering a psychotic episode. We were very close to her; she was like a daughter to us. We were shocked, devastated, saddened and gutted. How could we ever recover from this nightmare? Our son was arrested and the court eventually sentenced him to 15 years in jail, failed by the mental health system. We are 5 years on into the sentence, I say we, as a family we all have to do the time together to come out the other end. My wife and I visit him every weekend in jail.

I was introduced to happiness sweeping by my good friend Iggy Tan. I was a little unsure and awkward at first. But after a while I found that using the technique more often, then daily, I benefitted in work and my personal relationships. I can't control what happens with others, just being strong and positive is the best gift I can give them. Making happiness sweeping an everyday habit is a great reality check to bring you back in line. The sweeping has helped me to be much calmer; be in a positive frame of mind and able to cope with any pressures that arise. The sweeping practice has brought me to a better place. Moving forward I control what I can and I sweep away what I can't control. The mental anguish that I was suffering before is gone, replaced with a sense of calm, peace and clarity of the mind. My happiness level is an amazing 9/10 and still working for that 10/10, which I will get to! People are amazed at my happiness, peace and contentment level knowing what our family is going through. It is a miracle.

Chapter 4

THE SECRET TO HAPPINESS

MY QUEST AND DISCOVERY

As I mentioned in the Introduction, after suffering depression, I was curious with the question of whether people were able to reach 10/10 happiness, despite the very hectic environment we live in. I wondered if it was even possible in the chaos of today's modern society. My curiosity to answer these questions led me to commence my investigative journey on happiness.

DISCOVERY 1: HAPPINESS IS IN THE MIND

My journey started with the exploration of how people achieve a state of enlightenment, or 10/10 happiness. My first conclusion in this journey was a simple, profound truth: the gift of happiness truly lies within our mind. Happiness is not determined by what's happening around you, but rather what's happening inside your mind. Theoretically that made a lot of sense to me, so started the search for what in the mind determines or triggers happiness. You can choose to be happy but what in your mind is actually stopping you from making that choice? My search continued.

DISCOVERY 2: PEACE IN THE MIND
According to literature and ancient philosophy, peace in the mind creates happiness. A turbulent mind with lots of mental chatter prevents 10/10 happiness. At this point in my quest, I assumed that regular daily meditation would bring peace in the mind and then lead to 10/10 happiness. To my surprise this was not necessarily so. Whilst meditation brings an amount of contentment and peace in the mind of meditators, I discovered that something was still missing. Some long-term meditators still worry, stress and get frustrated. There was something else required to reach a worry-free enlightened state or 10/10 happiness. There must be another path to this elusive state, I thought.

DISCOVERY 3: CRAVINGS AND AVERSIONS
So what causes turbulence, unhappiness and suffering in the mind? Buddha was probably the first 'psychologist' who understood what affected peace in the mind and thus happiness. Buddhist philosophy states that cravings and aversions in our mind causes turbulence and mental suffering. Cravings are anything you want or desire and when it hasn't occurred or met your expectations, you get frustrated, you worry, stress and suffer mentally. Aversions are anything you push away, like fear, judgment, frustrations and anger. If you look deep into your life you realise that we have many cravings and aversions, leading to mental suffering and unhappiness. If you can reduce or rid yourself of these mental cravings and aversions, your suffering reduces and your happiness improves.

This made perfect sense to me but then I arrived at a fundamental issue. How do we get rid of cravings and aversions in our mind? In the ancient text it is said that Buddha meditated without moving from his seat for seven days, under a Ficus religiosa tree, to achieve this state of enlightenment. How can we achieve this in our modern lives? What is the secret?

DISCOVERY 4: ACCEPTANCE AND LETTING GO

I then discovered another ancient principle based on the idea that if you want to remove something you have to firstly know of its existence, accept it and then let it go. This is the practice of pure acceptance and letting go. So to remove a craving or aversion, I have to firstly identify it, accept it without judgement and then let it go. For example, when you accept the nature of the world as it is, you lose the craving to change it as well as everyone around you.

The next question was how to find a simple practice to facilitate this acceptance and letting go process. If it was not simple and easy to use, it wouldn't be incorporated in people's way of life and hence not sustainable. I also wanted something that would bypass the sabotaging nature of the Ego self. It came to me one morning and that's when I invented the happiness sweeping technique.

DISCOVERY 5: HAPPINESS SWEEPING

To my surprise, after regular sweeping, my cravings and aversions began to disappear and my mind was clearer, peaceful and contented. My happiness shot to 10/10. I didn't believe that I could actually be 10/10 happy with all the problems and stresses in my life. I was sceptical so I began trying out the technique on family, friends and colleagues. To my further amazement, people were feeling relief; they felt lighter and there were massive shifts in their happiness scores in just a very short period, often from just one session. I further refined the technique and the more I trialled it, the more the results surprised me. People were achieving 9 or 10 out of 10 happiness levels. What I discovered was that this happiness sweeping technique was like a powerful block preventing cravings/aversions to upset the peace in the mind.

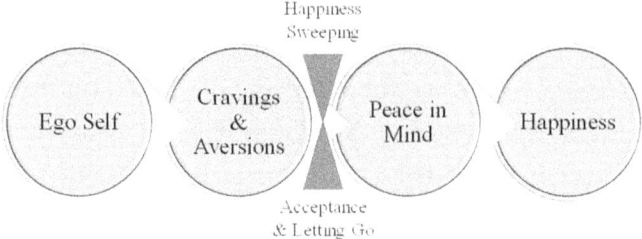

After gathering data from my work with 40 or more participants, I have observed dramatic increases in participants' happiness scores with an average improvement of 4 happiness points. In summary, 70 percent of participants who initially rated their happiness level as 'unhappy' shifted to 'very happy' after sustained happiness sweeping. The anecdotal data (see Chapter 7) indicates that happiness sweeping is a very powerful technique for dramatically shifting people's happiness levels quickly, as long as it is practised regularly. Eight participants achieved a score of 10/10 after sustained sweeping. At this point in my journey I thought perhaps this technique could also help people around the world be happier and more content. It might be bigger than just my group of 40 participants. Hopefully the unlimited sharing of the happiness sweeping technique can help with the greater good of humanity!

HAPPINESS IS IN THE MIND

Most people will agree with me that 'happiness' is an internal state of mind and not necessarily affiliated with the external environment. Yet we attach this 'happiness' to people, things and events, which is our external environment. You could be living in paradise but still be unhappy on the inside. But what about the people we know who face difficult circumstances yet still seem to be calm, have inner strength, peace and bliss? All of us have, or will have faced stress. We can't do anything about that but there is one thing we can control; the state of our mind. We know that happiness is a choice; but in the process of living in this world, we have confused 10/10 happiness with our satisfaction of the external environment.

"Even in the midst of disturbance, the stillness of the mind can offer sanctuary"

Stephen Richards

The first part to establishing happiness is to establish peace in your mind. Peace from the constant and unrelenting mind chatter of our Ego self. Peace from the mental suffering, worry, anxiety, frustration, envy and anger that impairs our mental well-being and creates unhappiness. Peace from the insistent cravings and fears that we'll never be able to truly satisfy. Once we have peace in the mind, we are on the path to attaining a contented and blissful life.

ACCEPTANCE THAT LIFE IS SUFFERING

One of the fundamental concepts of happiness relates to acceptance of life as imperfect and acceptance that suffering is just part of life. We suffer physically; we get sick; we grow old and we eventually die. Sounds a bit pessimistic, but accepting and not resisting this reality is how we can suffer less. It is the law of nature and embracing this truth helps us to 'let go' of the craving for a perfect, painless life. Every time life doesn't turn out the way we want, we have a craving for it not to have occurred and we suffer mentally.

The aversion towards pain, both physical and emotional, and the craving for pleasures is relentless. Each and every one of us suffers from dissatisfaction, fear, frustration, stress, anxiety and worry. Our mental suffering is one of the biggest threats to our well-being, especially today as the rates for depression, anxiety and suicide grow. Mental illness is becoming an epidemic.

GIVE UP CONTROL

Another part of acceptance is giving up trying to control everything and everyone around you; after all, you are just a single cell. Part of the beauty of life is that it's unpredictable. Nothing is permanent, everything changes and of course, a lot of things happen that can impact your life. If we want peace in our minds, there are in fact two options before us. One option is to try to change and control the nature of the world to suit our desires. Good luck with that. The second option is to change ourselves, our internal mind, so that we not only accept but also embrace the nature of the world as it is. This is, in essence, the practice of 'pure acceptance'.

Acceptance is the ability to truly be at peace with whatever comes your way and embrace it. Acceptance is the first realisation that you do not have control over everything. Trying to change the nature of the world has never worked for us in the past and unfortunately, will never work for us in the future. Despite this we are trapped in a constant, never-ending cycle of trying to control and change everything around us. This causes mental suffering.

> "People have a hard time letting go of their suffering. Out of a fear of the unknown, they prefer suffering that is familiar"
> Thich Nhat Hanh

We have to accept that undesirable events happen and have happened to us; they are happening right now and without doubt will continue to happen in the future. Acceptance is the process of embracing all of these events as a sweet part of your being. Acceptance is forgiveness and compassion. Forgive and be compassionate to yourself; forgive others; forgive the events of the past; forgive the events of the present; and even the future.

Perhaps two of the best examples of people practicing acceptance, forgiveness and letting go is Mahatma Ghandi and Nelson Mandela. Ghandi was the leader of the Indian independence movement against British rule. Employing non-violent civil disobedience, Ghandi led India to independence and inspired movements for civil rights and freedom across the world. Nelson Mandela is most widely recognised as the exemplar for love, acceptance and forgiveness. As the first South African president elected through a fully representative democratic election, Mandela galvanised his country to pursue a path of acceptance, forgiveness and reconciliation. He enabled the entire country to move past the numerous atrocities that occurred during the reign of apartheid. Having been subjected to a total of 27 years in prison, much of which he served on Robben Island, Mandela showed the world pure acceptance and letting go.

People may believe that acceptance means to give up or lose. You cannot necessarily change your situation so there are two ways out of the problem: accept what's happening, see the positives and choose a peaceful state of mind; or fight against it, be miserable and struggle against the universe. Until we master the art of acceptance, we will not have peace in our mind.

"My happiness grows in direct proportion to my acceptance and in inverse proportion to my expectations"
Michael J. Fox

Deepak Chopra, a new-age medical practitioner, describes how we need to receive, with open arms, what happens to us because if we fight and resist it, we generate a great deal of turbulence in our mind. He explains that we might want things to be different in the future, but in the present moment we need to accept things as they are. That's the way you can make your life flow smoothly instead of roughly.

LETTING GO

Acceptance and letting go are a part of the same process. Once you have identified the nature of the world as it is and realise that you cannot change nor control it, you can begin to 'let go'. So, by letting go, you internally 'let go' of the frustrations you have with your life. Let go of anger and bitterness. Let go of past issues with relationships. Let go of stress, worry and anxiety. Let go of attachments. For example, when we're worried, we are tightly attached to how we want things to be. When we're frustrated with someone, it's because we're attached to how we want them to be, rather than accepting them as they are.

Pamela Dussault, in her article *"Why, it is so hard to let go"* says that we have not really been taught to let go. *"The first step is the willingness to do so. The problem is that many people are genuinely not willing.*

They want to hold on for dear life and in most cases this is born from fear. In other cases, they may do so because they thrive on the drama, attention or power that holding on gives them".

The other area Dussault talks about is the lack of trust in life. "This is critical to letting go and often at the root of peoples' issues. 'Bad' things may have happened to you in the past – maybe even horrific ones. But the process of letting go is trusting that life will take you in the direction that is best for you in the long run. So know that you can choose to let go of the past and trust that life will take you to where you will truly be happy and joyful."

When we 'let go' of the Ego self, which is driving us to try to change the nature of the world, we exist in harmony with the nature of the world, resulting in internal peace, contentment and bliss.

"Let go a little, you will have a little peace.
If you let go a lot, you will have a lot of peace"
Ajahn Chah

According to Dr Judith Sills from Psychology Today, letting go means, "something has to open in your head and in your heart, but that shift, that easing, comes up against our own invisible, often implacable resistance. A great deal of that resistance comes from nothing more pedestrian than the great human reluctance to change. Even change for the better is still change, often initially dreaded and avoided".

Letting go has become somewhat of a cliché topic and is often used in all sorts of contexts. But it is the single most powerful skill we can cultivate in life. Nearly 2,500 years ago Buddha taught his followers about the power of changing their mental processes in order to alleviate emotional discomfort. Buddha taught us acceptance and letting go. This insight has since helped people free themselves from the patterns of thinking and behaving that perpetuate their suffering.

CRAVINGS AND AVERSIONS

Buddhist philosophy believes that cravings and aversions create mental suffering in the mind. A craving is defined as a desire that we long for or want greatly. We have conscious and subconscious cravings for many things such as success, wealth, material possessions, events, control, a certain image, etc. It is normal human behaviour to have cravings and desires. Unfortunately for each craving we don't satisfy, we suffer mentally. For example, if I have a craving for my teenage son to do well at school and he doesn't, I stress and worry, especially about his future. If he doesn't complete his homework, I get frustrated and angry with him. In the end, my happiness is adversely affected by having that craving. We all have constant cravings, many of which we are not even consciously aware of but the only outcome from having them is unfortunately mental suffering.

Aversions are defined as fear, frustration, hate, dislike, judgement and guilt. Like cravings, every aversion we have creates a little mental suffering. For example, my 'fear of failure' results in a lot of worry and anxiety when I perform an important job. My fear of not being able to pay the bills creates a lot of stress and worry, which adversely affects my happiness. My fears are based on external occurrences that haven't happened or are unlikely to happen, but they represent the greatest stress and anxiety in my mind. The collection of aversions, many of which we are unaware, add up to a great deal of subconscious mental suffering.

Some say cravings and aversions are generated from the Ego self. The Ego self fills your mind with the constant noisy chatter of criticism, self-doubt, worry, fear, jealousy, desires, frustrations and anger. These are all in the form of either a craving or aversion.

REDUCING CRAVINGS AND AVERSIONS

The ancient philosophy begins by saying that the cessation of cravings and aversions in the mind reduces suffering and increases our happiness. So removing cravings and aversions every day means our subconscious mind is ready to allow us to be 10/10 happy and thus live a truly happy life. This is a very simple truth that most people understand; but the fundamental challenge is how to reduce the cravings and aversions in our mind.

I believe that there is a misunderstanding about cessation of cravings. People have interpreted this idea as having to give up everything in their life; be celibate; and meditate under a tree in order to stop cravings and aversions. Let's face it, not many of us have the opportunity or the inclination to do that. Giving up a conventional life for a monastic one might help in reducing the temptation for cravings and aversions, but in the end I believe this can still be achieved in the mind, whilst carrying on with daily life. Remember, happiness is a state of mind and so is the cessation of cravings and aversions.

HAPPINESS SWEEPING

I have witnessed many people, who practise the Happiness Sweeping® technique daily, increase their inner happiness dramatically. These people have all sustained their state of happiness, despite the challenges and hardships they face. For example, Ashley (Chapter 2) has faced tremendous personal challenges with her two children both born with rare disorders. Her original happiness score was around 2-3 and sometimes even 0/10. Through daily happiness sweeping she now lives a peaceful and contented life with a happiness score of mostly 10/10. This doesn't mean she is impervious to what life throws at her, but she has the tools to quickly bring herself back to a high level of happiness. She has to constantly work at it to maintain her happiness as life has a tendency to throw non-stop curve balls. What has really helped her cope with life's challenges is the understanding that life is impermanent. Like a death of a friend, sickness of a loved one, a car accident, or a broken relationship, these examples demonstrate that life is in constant change. Ashley's mind is able to process events like these with a detached curiosity while acknowledging the impermanence of life.

Anguish in life is like a high-speed rollercoaster at a theme park. It's fast and often scary when it changes direction without your anticipation. You have no control of the rollercoaster so trying to control it will only cause you mental and physical harm. Those that embrace the rollercoaster ride without judgement, who move with the changes in direction and are present, are the ones that cope with life better. They're happy, peaceful and contented, despite the reckless ride. Ashley has attained a state of being where her happiness is an internal state of mind and not attached to people, things and events around her. She has achieved 'pure acceptance' and embraced the nature of the world as it is.

The next chapter is the book's most central as I introduce the happiness sweeping technique. All that is required is a quiet, private space where you can speak aloud without people thinking you have lost your mind! They still will!

Answers to your questions…

Q. If we were truly 10/10 happy, do we stop doing the things we do?

A. We have this idea that only unhappiness or dissatisfaction creates action or drive in us. We imagine enlightened people sitting under a tree somewhere for the rest of their lives. As I mention later in the book, life goes on and you will have the same passion and drive that you had before. The only difference is that there is no worry or attachment to the outcome. You don't just stop being passionate about what you believe in, be it climate change, world hunger, injustices, environmental degradation etc. You may recognise an injustice; you may decide to do something about it because you can. When you delay your happiness and attach it to the outcome then this becomes a problem. "I am happy today with the current threat of climate change"; "I am happy when I take action to help the threat of climate change". Either way, I still remain happy.

Q. How can you accept horrific past events?

A. Acceptance is not condoning the past events. Acceptance is recognising that you cannot change the past. It has happened and there is no right or wrong, good or bad. It is what it is. When we think something is unfair or unjust, we cannot let it go, we need justice. We want our enemies to suffer; we want them to apologise so they know how much hurt they have caused. This is very common and in the end basic to every human being on the planet. What we want is rarely ever going to happen yet we hang on so tightly to this desire that it affects our long-term happiness. Acceptance is only about your own happiness. In Chapter 8, I discuss blessing your enemies as a way to change this negative energy to positive energy and in doing so protecting your happiness.

Q. I tried but I just can't let go, what can I do?

A. You are no different to millions of human beings around the world. We all agree about the concept and benefit of acceptance and letting go, but how do we actually do it? Some painful past events are so emotionally-charged that it hurts too much to let go. That's why true happiness is so elusive. Through regular happiness sweeping you eventually get into a state where most of these painful past memories are accepted, embraced and they are no longer a source of suffering and unhappiness.

Q. Does letting go mean that you become detached, selfish and stop caring?

A. No; in actual fact, you become a different type of caring person. When you can do something about it, you will do everything you can to help those in need but you will stop mentally suffering for others. Mentally suffering for others does not change the outcome. You have no control of others' happiness. You will be sympathetic and caring but you will learn to detach from your loved one's sufferings. In the end, you become a more effective, caring person through your own acceptance, peacefulness, calmness and patience. Your internal happiness becomes your top priority.

Q. Why is it difficult to accept the 'Life is suffering' concept?

A. The concept is challenging because we are generally fearful of accepting that our life is full of hardships. We wish for a perfect fairy-tale life where we will live happily ever after. We are essentially fearful of becoming sick. We are fearful of getting old. We are fearful of suffering. We are fearful of death; not just for ourselves but for our loved ones that we leave behind. In order to accept and then let go of these fears we need to firstly embrace them; play, befriend and then send them along their way in the letting go process. We cannot accept our fears if we are not even willing to recognise them. Once again, through happiness sweeping, your fears begin to diminish.

Q. Can you really get rid of cravings forever?

A. The answer is no; they will return but each time they appear again it is with less and less intensity. Cravings can be reduced and dulled. Maybe someone in monastic practice has removed cravings forever but for the rest us we can only keep the cravings at bay by regular happiness sweeping. Cravings never fully disappear. We are human and cravings and aversions are part of our being. If we can quieten them with any mental technique then we can experience less suffering and more happiness.

 Tania's Story...

I'm a 55 year-old mother of two teenage daughters. Originally, my happiness score was a very low 2/10. I guess I was extremely unhappy and suffering terribly.

It was a couple of weeks before Christmas in 2016 I found out that I had breast cancer. This was a total shock to me as I am quite a healthy, clean living person. I wouldn't find out until after the operation on the 18 January, exactly the type of breast cancer and if had spread to any of my lymph nodes. I was pretty stressed and worried about the final results. I believe that stress caused my cancer and after the diagnosis, I had to get to a happier place in my life. I lost my job and my husband was also out of work. I had big issues to deal with in regards to my teenage daughter. I had to change my mindset to get through this challenging time in my life and beyond. With both of us out of work, we were really struggling as a family. This was probably the worst period in our lives. I was certainly distressed and desperate.

Quite a while before my diagnosis, I had spoken to a great friend of mine, whom had mentioned she was doing some mind sweeping and meditation, which had really helped her with her her own problems and stress. She thought it would be a good idea for me to try the technique to get me through my cancer. I was sceptical at first. She organised for me to contact Iggy Tan whom called me about a week after my diagnosis. Iggy stepped me through the process of the happiness sweeping technique over the phone and organised for me to meet him a couple of weeks later. So began the daily routine of sweeping practice. I must say initially I thought it was strange, but having already practised meditation over the years, I found it easy to achieve. I have continued to do the sweeping several times a day, usually when

I am walking my dog in the morning and then just before bed; as well as when I am stressed during the day. I also find walking around my back yard doing the sweeping technique is effective as I am able to talk out loud (and at times scream). Hearing the words actually really helps to make it real to me; and getting all the negatives off my chest is cleansing. So, after speaking with Iggy, over the following 6 weeks, I focussed on sweeping, meditating and eating a very healthy diet to achieve better levels of happiness. With the help of my wonderful husband, daughters and friends who kept me occupied; plus resting when I wasn't sleeping, I achieved a great result.

I would say I did feel a lot better leading up to the operation and I felt completely calm being wheeled into the operating room. I can remember all my friends coming to visit me afterwards, all commenting 'you look amazing' and 'you have a glow'. I put this down to the regular sweeping and meditation. I felt so positive I was bursting. I still had to wait another 13 days before I had my final results but I had a great feeling everything would be okay.

On 31 January I was given the all clear; I was cancer free and feeling on top of the world. I was still dealing with the shock of what had happened over the last couple of months; and anxiety had reared its ugly head. This arises every now and again. I am continuing to do my happiness sweeping to help me get through my life's challenges.

After a period of time, my happiness shot to an amazing 7 out of 10 and at times 8 out of 10. I am meditating daily and I go to a class with likeminded people. Iggy is always there for me if I need to talk about how I am feeling and to get me to a better happiness level too.

I think the main thing I am getting out of the happiness sweeping and meditation is that it forces you to just let things go, all the little things that bother you on a daily basis. I am calmer and less anxious, thus creating a happiness within, a kind of blissful feeling deep inside. I know I will be continuing to practise this process as I feel it has become a part of my life in a very positive way; and I still feel there is always room for further improvement.

I would say to someone wanting to give it a go, please do so. You will notice a significant difference in your health, attitude and happiness. I don't know how I would have coped with the recent events of my life without the introduction of happiness sweeping. If it feels strange to begin with, keep trying and it will eventually become clear when you see the results.

Chapter 5

HAPPINESS SWEEPING®

HAPPINESS SWEEPING

In this chapter we cover the happiness sweeping technique. It is important to sit somewhere private and quiet while reading this chapter, as you might want to speak aloud during the sweeping session without potentially being judged.

The sweeping technique is a very simple process that first involves identifying each craving in your mind (this is the process of accepting) and once identified physically throwing the craving away (as part of the 'letting go' process). Often we are ashamed, or even guilty, of having certain cravings. We don't want to admit the craving to ourselves or to someone else; like a craving to be rich, successful or more attractive. Identifying each craving without judgement of yourself is the process of pure acceptance. For example, having to admit that you have a craving for a larger house, which could be considered materialistic and shallow. But this admission process allows you to acknowledge the craving without any judgement; tell yourself that it is okay to have a craving for a new house. It is being compassionate to yourself. Once you have identified and acknowledged each craving, it is time to let these cravings go, again without judgement or analysis. The physical act of throwing each craving away is a symbolic act that assists with the process of letting go.

STEP 1. SWEEP AWAY CRAVINGS

The first step is to identify a craving (without judgement) in your subconscious mind. Then once identified, say it aloud using the words **"my craving *to be successful*…"**, while physically grabbing the figurative craving and sweeping it from your head using your hand.

In the same motion, throw the craving away with the corresponding throwing away action while saying "…**is gone**" to complete the sentence. "**My craving *to be successful* is gone.**"

The physical hand gestures – grabbing, sweeping and throwing away – are important for the 'letting go' process.

Important Note: *Please ensure you follow the steps in order to develop the technique effectively. Remember to say the craving aloud and then physically sweep, grab and throw away. A visual example of the Happiness Sweeping® technique is available on YouTube:* ***www.youtube.com/happinesssweeping*** *(Happiness Sweeping: Stop Craving Happiness)*

*The sweeping hand action is important as it symbolises the sweeping out of dirty, negative-energy from your subconscious mind, while you verbalise what it is you are sweeping away. If the technique is carried out only in the mind without the physical actions, it will not work as effectively. Please do not try to overthink the exercise; just do it without judgement; there is no right or wrong way. Do not try to reason or justify why you should hold onto each individual craving or aversion; be open, trust the process and 'let go', no matter how deep or trivial. You need to **'let go'** to improve your happiness.*

Please start sweeping your cravings away using the next few examples to help you on your way. Own it and emotionally let it go.

CRAVINGS (EXAMPLES)

- *My craving to be liked is gone.*
- *My craving to be financially secure is gone.*
- *My craving to be perfect is gone.*
- *My craving to pay all my bills is gone.*
- *My craving to be in a good relationship is gone.*
- *My craving to be a good parent is gone.*
- *My craving to be rich is gone.*
- *My craving to lose weight is gone.*

It is at this point where you might be telling yourself that you don't actually want to throw away your craving to lose weight, for example, because you *do* want to lose weight. Remember, letting go of the craving doesn't mean that it will stop you from achieving a goal, or stop you from actually losing weight, in this example. It just removes the anxious or negative feelings surrounding the craving. Remember, you are happy if you lose weight and you are equally happy if you don't lose weight.

- *My craving to exercise more is gone.*
- *My craving to be right all the time is gone.*
- *My craving for my child to do well at school is gone.*
- *My craving to be accepted is gone.*
- *My craving to get a promotion at work is gone.*
- *My craving for more sex is gone.*
- *My craving for more money is gone.*
- *My craving to be loved and cherished is gone.*
- *My craving for my friend to recover from cancer is gone.*
- *My craving for my parent to be back on this earth is gone.*

Now over to you; with reflection, start identifying your mind's cravings. Only you can identify your deep desires and cravings. It is important to reflect *deeply* to access the underlying cravings that have plagued your subconscious for long periods of time and 'let go'. Be genuine, raw and true to yourself. Take it seriously.

- *My craving for ………….. is gone.*
- *My craving for ………….. is gone.*
- *My craving for ………….. is gone.*

STEP 2. SWEEP AWAY AVERSIONS

The next step is identifying your aversions and sweeping them away without judgement. The three strongest aversions we have are fear, worry and frustration.

AVERSIONS (FEAR)

- *My fear of being on my own is gone.*
- *My fear of losing my job is gone.*
- *My fear of being judged is gone.*
- *My fear of dying and leaving my loved ones is gone.*
- *My fear of getting sick is gone.*
- *My fear of my parents dying is gone.*
- *My fear of not being able to pay my bills is gone.*
- *My fear of getting depression one day is gone.*
- *My fear of flying is gone.*
- *My fear of my marriage failing is gone.*
- *My fear of having a poor relationship with my child is gone.*

Now, try your own fears (take your time to reflect first). Sometimes these are deep fears that you have never acknowledged to yourself nor anyone else. Once identified, acknowledge and let go. Once again, like the sweeping away of cravings, be genuine, raw and authentic – and as always, please take your time.

- *My fear of ……………. is gone.*
- *My fear of ……………. is gone.*
- *My fear of ……………. is gone.*

Now let's start to sweep away the worries you have in your mind.

AVERSIONS (WORRY)

- *My worry about my lack of physical fitness is gone.*
- *My worry about getting old is gone.*
- *My worry about my son not achieving in school is gone.*
- *My worry about not being accepted is gone.*
- *My worry about my lack of motivation is gone.*

- *My worry about not having enough time is gone.*
- *My worry about …………… is gone.*

Now let's start to sweep away the frustrations you have in your mind.

AVERSIONS (FRUSTRATION)

- *My frustration for people gossiping at work is gone.*
- *My frustration for my child avoiding homework is gone.*
- *My frustration for my child not cleaning their room is gone.*
- *My frustration for my wife nagging me is gone.*
- *My frustration at myself for not coping is gone.*
- *My frustration towards my boss is gone.*
- *My frustration of ……………... is gone.*
- *My frustration of ……………... is gone.*

RESULT AFTER SWEEPING

Now that you have completed a full sweeping session, you might feel a bit lighter, like a load has been lifted from you. You may feel a bit stupid or awkward at first. If there is no change, then don't worry as it will come with more practise. If you feel lighter then this is a result of just 2-3 minutes of sweeping you have just completed. Imagine what you would feel like if you did this regularly? After their first attempt, some of the participants described an immediate feeling of a burden being lifted figuratively from their shoulders. One participant had an original happiness score of 0/10 and after her first session she shifted to 7/10. She cried with emotion as she swept each craving and aversion away, which her subconscious mind had held onto for decades.

In some of our previous happiness sessions I have asked participants to turn to look at the person next to them; and in front of a complete stranger, practise the happiness sweeping technique. Facing each other, participants would take turns sweeping. The fear of being judged dissipated; it was such a wonderful feeling for all. After the exercise we realised that, in the end, we are all human beings carrying around the same mental sufferings and the same imperfections as each other. It is an intense feeling of relief when you realise that each one of us is not necessarily unique and we all actually experience very similar mental sufferings.

SWEEP YOUR MIND EVERY DAY

The cravings and aversions we just swept away unfortunately will return to our subconscious mind the next day. So, in order to maintain the effect, we need to sweep twice every day plus additional sweeping if and when required. Some people feel happy after their first or second sweep, but then forget to sweep again. Maintenance and upkeep is of key importance.

We all brush our teeth twice a day, normally without fail. We do this to protect our teeth from bacteria and plaque to maintain oral health. Similarly, we also need to clean our subconscious mind from 'nasties' twice a day to maintain our happiness. Brush your teeth, sweep your mind. It is the daily purification of your mind. Some participants tell me they sweep while in the toilet or in the shower. Some sweep in the car while driving to and from work. Whatever place and time that works best for you is great; the most important thing is to make it a habit.

Have you heard of the 21/90 rule of thumb? According to the theory, if you practise something every day for 21 days it will become a habit. If you practise something for 90 days it will become a lifestyle. I guarantee that you will get a sustained improvement in your happiness score if you make daily sweeping a lifestyle.

SWEEP THOUGHTS OF THE PAST AND FUTURE AWAY

The Ego self loves to dwell on the past or become preoccupied with the future. If you have thoughts about the past or the future, it is usually in the form of a craving or aversion. For example, *"I wish that I didn't change my job three years ago"*. This thought is a craving for something to not have happened in the past. Sweep it away. Another example, *"If I don't get a promotion by next year, I won't be able to afford a holiday"*; this is a fear of something potentially not happening. Sweep it away.

Eckhart Tolle, author of the *Power of Now* believes that we replay past mistakes repeatedly in our mind, allowing feelings of shame and regret to shape our actions in the present. *"We cling to frustration and we worry about the future, as if the act of fixation somehow gives us power. We hold stress in our minds and bodies, potentially creating serious health issues and accept that state of tension as the norm"*.

Living in the moment means letting go of the past and not waiting for the future. It means living consciously, aware that each moment you breathe is a gift.

Oprah Winfrey

Once you are aware that every thought you have of the past or the future is a craving or aversion, you can sweep it away. The past and future chatter in your mind begins to slow and you start living in the present. Clarity of the mind will then ensue.

- *My craving to be promoted before my 40ᵗʰ birthday is gone (future)*
- *My fear of losing my job next year is gone (future)*
- *My craving for justice for my marriage breakdown is gone (past)*
- *My frustration for regreting my career path after I left university is gone (past)*

BLESS YOUR ENEMIES

The Ego self also loves holding onto grudges and blame to justify our unhappiness. When someone frustrates or angers you, your energy becomes negative and you feel sad and unhappy. You want revenge and justice. Most of us can recall events or people from our past that have caused us suffering. Just a memory of a certain person from your past right now might even alter your current mood. Can you see that this type of negative thought is just a craving or aversion? A craving for events not to have happened; a craving for that person to admit fault; a craving for justice; and perhaps a craving for an end to the suffering? The aversion is fear, perhaps; fear of the person causing you more harm; fear of events occurring again; fear of your mental well-being. So, to deal with the negative effects from having this thought of the past, sweep the associated cravings and aversions away as per the happiness sweeping technique. *"My craving for that painful situation not to have happened is gone"; "My craving for justice is gone."* etc. Once you have swept them away, your energy requires a change from negative to positive energy; this is through blessing the person. Yes, bless (not from a religious point of view) by wishing or projecting loving kindness and compassion to the person/s who caused you suffering.

Think of the person/s and wish them positive sentiments (aloud if you like). Raising your hands, think of them, bless them (feel the love energy leave from your hands) with lots of peace, abundance, happiness, prosperity and compassion. Feel the positive energy shift from your hands towards them. Wish them joy and loving kindness; and this starts the process of taming your Ego self.

BLESSING (EXAMPLES)

- *"I bless and wish John lots of peace and happiness"*
- *"I bless and wish John prosperity and abundance"*
- *"I bless and wish John lots of joy and compassion"*
- *"I bless and wish John every success for the future"*
- *"I bless and wish John good health and a good life"*
- *"I bless and wish John a blissful and fufilled life"*

Throughout the daily interactions with people we might encounter someone who makes us feel frustrated, angry or embarrassed. For example, someone who has hurt you emotionally; physically abused you; bullied you at work; embarrassed you in front of fellow colleagues; or stolen your parking spot. Change the energy to positive energy straight away by blessing the person. The onus is on you to always keep your happiness intact; remembering that you can't control anyone else.

MASTERING THE SWEEPING AND BLESSING

Once you are comfortable with routinely sweeping in the morning and evening each and every day, start using the technique more often. If a stressful or undesirable event arises, sweep the cravings and aversions associated with the event immediately. Even by doing a quick sweep every now and then, you can create a nice solid shield for maintaining your happiness throughout the day.

Here is an example:

I get an email at work from a colleague (John) who I believe has done the wrong thing because he missed an agreed deadline. I feel upset and angry; my mood and happiness starts to become affected. I am worried about missing the deadline. I am frustrated. After reading John's email I start to internally identify the cravings and aversions associated with this occurrence and begin sweeping.

- *My craving for John to be more considerate is gone.*
- *My craving to be in the right all the time is gone.*
- *My craving to control John's actions is gone.*
- *My craving to meet all agreed deadlines is gone.*
- *My fear of John causing me to look bad is gone.*
- *My fear of our relationship deteriorating is gone.*
- *My frustration for John not understanding me is gone.*
- *My frustration of John's sub standard work is gone.*

In this example, by sweeping away all the cravings and aversions associated with this single event I am able to bring myself back to a contented state. I would also bless John by providing loving kindness and compassionate blessings (positive energy) to him. As a result, I am now much calmer than before, more peaceful and my anger has dissipated. I realise that I cannot change the past; the event has happened. I now have to deal with the consequences of John's mistake and prevent it from happening again. So within a few minutes of reading the email, I am totally calm, neutral and have handled the situation without my happiness being affected. I have managed to detach myself from the external event to prevent it from affecting my inner happiness. Rather than blaming John, I have chosen to take full responsibility for maintaining my happiness, in spite of adverse external conditions. I have accepted the situation and have let go of all the fears, anger and anxiety straight away. Don't wait until you get home to sweep; it is better to not let it affect you at the time. Yes, it takes a bit of mental effort and sweeping but the protection of your inner happiness is the reward.

The acceptance of the situation with John does not mean that I have just accepted his sub-standard effort and covered for him. I plan to deal with John's poor performance but I will be approaching him from a peaceful state of mind rather than an angry, uncontrolled one. Which inner state would allow more effective communication and resolution?

PERFORMANCE ENHANCEMENT

Happiness sweeping is a powerful tool to enhance and improve performance in all areas of your life. Whether it is in sport, acting, cooking, singing, washing your car, entertaining, public speaking or even in the bedroom.

For example, you are about to give a presentation to a public audience; let's face it, your mind is already filled with cravings and aversions. This is often felt as nervousness or butterflies in your stomach. It is essentially a mild form of anxiety fuelled by cravings to do well and fear of not meeting expectations. As a CEO, my job involves presenting investment pitches to private or public investors. I am fairly comfortable with presenting and public speaking, however, before I go up on stage what do you think is going on inside my head? No matter how experienced the speaker, there will always be a bunch of cravings and aversions sitting inside the subconscious mind. So I start sweeping before its show time:

- *"My craving to make a good presentation is gone"*
- *"My craving for the audience to like my pitch is gone"*
- *"My craving to impress the audience is gone"*
- *"My fear of not being accepted is gone"*
- *"My fear of not doing a good job is gone"*
- *"My fear of being judged is gone"*

After sweeping I feel totally at ease and ready to proceed to the stage. What I find is that I am totally present with the audience; there is no interfering mental chatter going on in my head and I am able to deliver a good performance as a result. People have commented about how 'in the zone' I seem while presenting. I also enjoy the experience so much more without the limiting and critical Ego self chattering away in the background. In this way, happiness sweeping is also very effective for sport. I practise sweeping when playing golf and have had the best golf rounds ever since. This is called 'flow'.

IN THE FLOW

Mihalyi Csikszentmihalyi, a Hungarian psychologist, is one of the pioneers of 'flow' research. His initial studies focused on creative individuals but his concepts actually apply to all people, creative or not. In his book, *Flow* (1990), he describes the idea as being consciously in inner harmony with whatever you're doing. He contends that *"happiness connects to our ability to feel flow in our lives and that it must be cultivated and practised. At times, however, flow occurs by chance when certain experiences converge"*. For example, you might be at a dinner party and strike up a conversation with someone and find that you have a common interest, which leads you to have lunch, which then turns into a joint business venture months later. This is a merging of action and a state of awareness. Being open-minded and being a good listener is an important aspect of flow. Happiness sweeping will help you be more present in everything you do. You can use this technique for anything and you will produce much better results and enjoy the whole experience so much more.

HAPPINESS STOCKTAKE

So at this point, right this second, what is your inner happiness score out of ten? One (1) being the least happy, ten (10) being enlightened. Go on, write in your score:

My score:

Has your score improved now that you have completed a sweeping session? If it has, then this should convince you of the benefit of the practice. If you haven't moved on your happiness score, keep reflecting deeply and keep practising. It will come.

SUMMARY CHECKLIST
- ☐ *PRACTISE HAPPINESS SWEEPING DAILY*
- ☐ *SWEEP PAST AND FUTURE CRAVINGS & AVERSIONS*
- ☐ *BLESS YOUR ENEMIES*

Answers to your questions…

Q. Do I have to do the physical sweep hand action and say it aloud?

A. The short answer is yes. If you are at first worried about people thinking you are crazy, then find a quiet spot to do your sweeping. I believe the physical hand and throwing action is particularly important as it bypasses the mind where the Ego self can sabotage the process. Some participants have also described feeling a 'dirty ball of energy' in their hands, from their mind, that they then throw away. I often sweep under the table during a meeting when I start to get agitated or frustrated. This is part of being mindful of your happiness state all the time.

Q. Do I have to raise my hands when blessing my enemies?

A. The blessing hand action allows the flow of peace and loving kindness energy to move from your hands towards the imagined person. This energy release from your hands creates a circuit for new peace and loving kindness energy to move through you. That's the reason you feel more calm and peaceful after blessing. Try to suspend your judgement and give it a go for yourself.

Q. Do I have to bring up events of my past, which I believe may have been suppressed?

A. The answer is absolutely, yes. We all have suppressed past occurrences filled with hurt and pain, which we buried deep in our subconscious. On occasions flashes of memories come up and create suffering and unhappiness. To be at a higher level of happiness we need to purge this painful past. Often your Ego self is also fearful of addressing painful memories. The past has already happened and cannot hurt you anymore yet we are still so fearful of it. Essentially we are fearful of reliving the pain; fearful of forgiving ourselves and the people that have caused us hurt. The pain of the past needs to be embraced. It needs to be felt, touched and befriended in a purely non-judgemental and compassionate way. Use the blessing technique described in this chapter to forgive your enemies and maintain your happiness level.

Q. Do I sweep more often than twice a day?

A. Yes of course. In fact, to get people into the practice I recommended a minimum of just twice a day. Participants that are proficient at regular sweeping then start to carry it out throughout their day. If you get frustrated, stressed or angry, recognise it immediately and sweep it away before it is allowed to affect your happiness. This is the ultimate level of mindfulness. You become mindful of your thoughts but importantly how your thoughts affect your happiness level. If happiness affects all aspects of your life including your health, longevity, productivity, creativity, relationships and mental well-being, WHAT ELSE IS MORE IMPORTANT?

 Jade's Story...

My name is Jade and my happiness score was initially around 3/10. With a score of 3, I guess I wasn't happy at all. At the time I had just come out of a 13 year abusive relationship where I had developed severe anxiety to the point of having to be medicated. I had also started to become a recluse to some extent as I had lost my sense of self-worth and confidence. This was due to being told by my husband that I was not intelligent, not capable of doing anything for myself and even down to not disciplining our 7 year-old daughter correctly.

My ex-husband would talk down to me in company and a lot of our friends had seen how he was to me; but as he was so nice to everyone else; and such a good dad to our daughter, they didn't really believe the extent of the mental abuse I was suffering. Finally I got the courage to tell him to leave and he attacked me physically; he tried to strangle me. I moved out and never went back. I lost all our friends of 13 years as he convinced them that it was me who was insane. Because most of them were his childhood friends they stuck by him. I struggled to let go of this as I thought how could people support someone who was mentally and physically abusive to his wife. I was angry and in some ways wanted revenge and that anger started to consume me.

I have worked with Iggy professionally for many years. As a friend he kindly introduced me to the sweeping technique. I had been doing mindfulness therapy for two years prior – I think that's what gave me the initial courage to leave my husband. I was unhappy and suffered from anxiety and anger.

At first it was hard to get into the routine of sweeping and as Iggy says every day these thoughts creep back in. This meant my progress was slow, at first. Today it's just a way of life. Sweeping is the last thing I do at night to enable a less-troubled night's sleep. It is also the first thing in the morning, especially if I wake up with things on my mind. Generally I also sweep during the day when negative thoughts and feelings creep in.

It might seem strange at first but the benefits are endless. I'm still not settled with my ex-husband financially and still struggle to pay the bills. I cope with everyday life challenges, especially with running my own business and having a school-aged daughter.

But I'm at peace with myself and with my circumstances. I'm the happiest and calmest I've ever been in my life. My happiness score sits at 9/10 consistently and people have commented on how happy I am. They all want whatever I am taking!

Chapter 6

HOW EFFECTIVE IS HAPPINESS SWEEPING?

WHAT ARE THE RESULTS?

The big questions are, does happiness sweeping work and if so, is it sustainable? The only way to answer these questions is to explore the results of forty (40) participants that have undertaken happiness sweeping by incorporating it into their everyday lives. Note that the evidence is merely anecdotal; the data is based on my personal tracking of each participant's happiness score before and after the implementation. It's heavily biased, and it's not a randomised controlled group or a empirical study, but the results are still interesting.

Each participant's happiness score was listed into five categories (my definition) as detailed in Table 1. The categorisation process was based on the participant's assessment of their own happiness level: distressed (0-2), unhappy (3-5), happy (6-7), very happy (8-9) and enlightened (10).

> "Most people are about as happy as they make up their minds to be."
>
> Abraham Lincoln

Table 1 – Categorisation of happiness levels

Happiness Score Range	My Category
0 - 2	Distressed
3 - 5	Unhappy
6 - 7	Happy
8 - 9	Very Happy
10	Enlightened

Before being introduced to the happiness sweeping technique, the participants' happiness scores ranged from 0 to 8 with an average score of 4.4 overall and a standard deviation of 2.0. The data is presented in Table 2.

Table 2 – Happiness score before and after sustained happiness sweeping

Participant Ref	Before Sweeping	After Sweeping	Gain	Participant Ref	Before Sweeping	After Sweeping	Gain
A	4	9	5	V	2	8	6
B	4	9	5	W	5	8	3
C	3	9	6	X	5	9	4
D	3	8	5	Y	0	8	8
E	5	8	3	Z	4	5	1
F	7	10	3	AA	3	10	7
G	7	9	2	AB	5	8	3
H	5	10	5	AC	7	10	3
I	5	9	4	AD	1	8	7
J	6	10	4	AE	0	6	6
K	3	9	6	AF	5	8	3
L	8	10	2	AG	2	6	4
M	6	10	4	AH	2	9	7
N	6	9	3	AI	4	8	4
O	6	9	3	AJ	6	9	3
P	4	8	4	AK	4	9	5
Q	5	8	3	AL	4	7	3
R	2	7	5	AM	6	10	4
S	3	8	5	AN	6	9	3
T	5	8	3	Average	4.4	8.5	4.2
U	7	9	2	Std Dev	2.0	1.2	1.7

Out of the forty (40) participants, only one (1) participant had an original happiness score classified in the 'very happy' category (participant 'L' was an 8/10) before embarking on happiness sweeping. Participant L was a long-term meditation practitioner and after her first happiness sweeping session she reached 10/10 happiness.

Table 2 also shows each participant's happiness score after a period of time (ranging from a period of 1 month to 24 months) after first being introduced to happiness sweeping. The overall average score for the entire group was 8.5, which is an overall average improvement of 4.2 points. The biggest happiness score improvement was from three (3) participants 'Y', 'AD' and 'AH'; all were originally in category 1 'distressed' (happiness scores 0, 1, and 2 out of 10) and after being introduced to the technique recorded scores of 8, 8 and 9 ('very happy') respectively. The overall summary is presented in Table 3 and the data is also presented in Figures 1 and 2.

Table 3 – Overall Results Summary

Happiness Score Range	Category	Participants Before HS	Participants After HS
0 - 2	Distressed	7	0
3 - 5	Unhappy	21	1
6 - 7	Happy	11	4
8 - 9	Very Happy	1	27
10	Enlightened	0	8
	Total	40	40
Percentage	Unhappy	70%	3%
	Happy	28%	10%
	Very Happy	3%	68%
	Enlightened	0%	20%

Figure 1 - Happiness score distribution before happiness sweeping

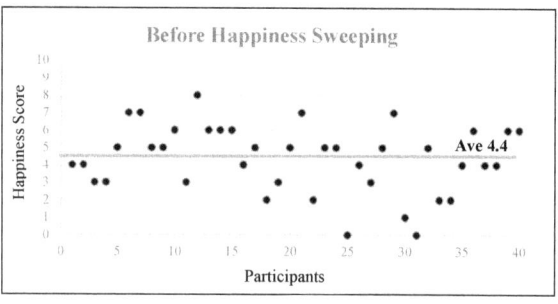

Figure 2 - Happiness score distribution after happiness sweeping

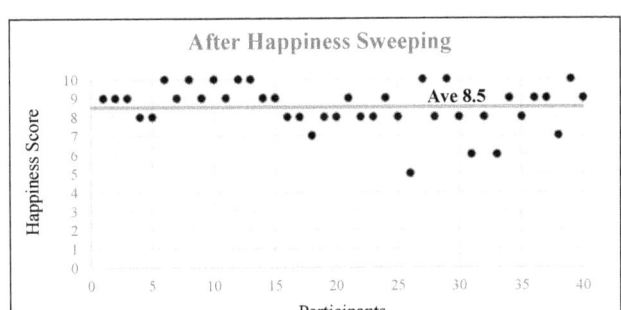

Before being introduced to the happiness sweeping technique, seventy (70) percent of participants rated their happiness level equivalent to the 'unhappy' category (score 3, 4 or 5), while twenty eight (28) percent considered themselves corresponding to the 'happy' category (score 6 or 7). After continuing to practise happiness sweeping for a period of time, sixty eight (68) percent of the participants reported their happiness level as 'very happy' (score 8 or 9). Out of forty (40) participants 20 percent (8 participants) rated their happiness score at 10/10 after implementing the technique on a continuous basis.

So is the improvement in the participants' happiness scores significant from a statistical point of view? Statistically significant testings (t (39) =15.8, p<0.05) shows that the average improvement of 4.2 points in a happiness score is significant at a 95 percent confidence level. This means there is strong evidence that the improvement in happiness is valid and significant. The analysis suggests that happiness sweeping, if practised regularly, will result in an overall mean improvement of happiness that is considered statistically significant.

Throughout the study I also noticed that the improvement in a happiness score is not necessarily a linear relationship. In other words, to shift your happiness score from a 2 to a 6 is much easier than trying to get from a 7 to a 9, for example. To move from a 9 to a 10 is also a challenge.

CONCLUSION

The anecdotal results indicate that happiness sweeping is a very powerful technique for dramatically shifting people's happiness levels quickly towards 10; as long as it is practised regularly. Eighty eight (88) percent of the participants reported amazing final happiness scores of 8, 9 or 10. The majority of participants reported less worry and stress as well as increased levels of peace and contentment. In addition, they also claim that their 'mental chatter' is quieter, to the point where there is complete clarity in the mind and their intuition is heightened. Most of the group reported less cravings for material and external desires; and fears had subsided dramatically. Nothing makes them angry or frustrated in the same way anymore. A common trend with all the participants is that nearly all believe that they were more present and less worried about the past or the future after implementing regular happiness sweeping. Interestingly, out of the eight (8) participants on a score of 10/10 (after happiness sweeping) half (4) were also practicing regular meditation (loving kindness and compassion meditation) in addition to the happiness sweeping. The other half (4 participants) reached 10/10 by happiness sweeping alone, without meditation. So it is possible to achieve 10/10 happiness just by happiness sweeping.

Answers to your questions…

Q. Does everyone in my own family use the happiness sweeping technique?

A. Only my eldest son; he uses happiness sweeping on a regular basis. Through sweeping he has recovered from depression and anxiety and is no longer on medication. He sweeps regularly and is able to maintain a happiness level of 10/10. He initially refused to even consider the technique. Remember, trying to get someone to do something that might be potentially good for them is still a craving. It is absolutely okay that some choose not to take up the happiness sweeping and some do. You can lead a horse to water but you can't make it drink. Craving for the horse to drink water makes you unhappy so you have to look after your happiness and let go.

Q. When I am happy, why do I feel guilty when I am around unhappy people?

A. When I see other members of my family suffer with bouts of unhappiness, sadness and anguish with their normal life's challenges, I can become frustrated and angry. Frustrated because they are not helping themselves with a technique that works; but once again these are my cravings. I sweep the cravings for them to be happy, the cravings for them not to suffer and then sweep the frustrations that they are not using the happiness sweeping technique to help themselves. By doing this, I look after my personal happiness and detach from the notion that I can influence their happiness. Of course if there is something I can physically do to help them, I am happy to help without judgement. I don't try to change anything about them but just try to be there alongside them while they're suffering. I can still be 10/10 happy and be there, holding their hand. I don't have to feel guilty about it. There is no rule in life that says you have to suffer for others. It doesn't change the outcome. In fact, being peaceful, non-judgemental, focused and being there for them in their space is more beneficial.

Q. Does a person's happiness improve when you're around?

A. What is amazing is that by osmosis, people close to me become happier. As I mentioned before, only my son uses the happiness sweeping technique. However, through osmosis (the process of gradual or unconscious assimilation), my daughter and other son have hit 10/10 happiness without the daily sweeping. The others are at 8/10. My daughter says that she may have taken the concepts on mentally without actually doing the sweeping. Whatever way you choose to practise compassion, acceptance and letting go, your happiness will improve.

Q. Does the happiness sweeping help with anger management?

A. Anger is when the world, people, behaviours and events do not meet your judgemental view of how things should be. The world as it is does not match how the world should be in your mind. You lose your patience, it causes your body to release adrenaline, your muscles tighten, and your heart rate and blood pressure to increase. You have two choices; continue to try to change the world and be frustrated and angry throughout the process; or accept the world as it is and be happy and at peace. Happiness sweeping is the ultimate anger management strategy.

Lesley's Story...

My name's Lesley. I'm a 55 year-old retired school teacher. I am a long term Twin Hearts meditation practitioner.

I'd say that I'm a reasonable and caring person. Well, at least most of the time. One day though, I happened to be conversing with Iggy and I mentioned that I wasn't really 100 percent happy. Nothing really major but it was the little things that were adding up. Stress, time management, not happy with the way certain family relationships were going and issues with weight. Also, a lot of unresolved issues would constantly surface in my mind. In spite of this, I would stay on a 6/10 or 7/10. Not bad but not fulfilling either!

Over a coffee, Iggy explained the sweeping technique to me. I was familiar with it because it's the same technique that's used to remove diseased energy in energy healing. I was aware that this works! I tried it a bit while at the café and found myself feeling much lighter already. Somehow, that feeling of heaviness in the head had gone! Just like that! Wow! I had an indescribable clarity, like a fog had lifted from my mind. My happiness lifted straight away to 9/10 and I was amazed. Immediately, I felt more contented and a sense of peace.

As suggested by Iggy, I started doing this fairly regularly. Any desire or aversion was removed. Initially, I would do it at bedtime when reflecting on my day. Now, I can identify a thought immediately and categorise it as either a desire or an aversion. Also, I can catch it and sweep it away before it settles into my mind.

This technique has made me much more aware of my thought processes. As a result, I'm calmer and I feel more in control of my emotions. I can look at life from a third person's point of view. This has also developed in me a sense of being non-judgemental and seeing people, things and situations for how they really are and not coloured by my emotions!

My personal biggest advantage and achievement now is that there is no sense of worry, anxiety or fear. Nothing to win or lose! My score now is a fantastic 10 most of the time. I truly want to thank Iggy for this technique. Certainly a life-changing one!!

Lesley's Story…

My name's Lesley. I'm a 55 year-old retired school teacher. I am a long term Twin Hearts meditation practitioner.

I'd say that I'm a reasonable and caring person. Well, at least most of the time. One day though, I happened to be conversing with Iggy and I mentioned that I wasn't really 100 percent happy. Nothing really major but it was the little things that were adding up. Stress, time management, not happy with the way certain family relationships were going and issues with weight. Also, a lot of unresolved issues would constantly surface in my mind. In spite of this, I would stay on a 6/10 or 7/10. Not bad but not fulfilling either!

Over a coffee, Iggy explained the sweeping technique to me. I was familiar with it because it's the same technique that's used to remove diseased energy in energy healing. I was aware that this works! I tried it a bit while at the café and found myself feeling much lighter already. Somehow, that feeling of heaviness in the head had gone! Just like that! Wow! I had an indescribable clarity, like a fog had lifted from my mind. My happiness lifted straight away to 9/10 and I was amazed. Immediately, I felt more contented and a sense of peace.

As suggested by Iggy, I started doing this fairly regularly. Any desire or aversion was removed. Initially, I would do it at bedtime when reflecting on my day. Now, I can identify a thought immediately and categorise it as either a desire or an aversion. Also, I can catch it and sweep it away before it settles into my mind.

This technique has made me much more aware of my thought processes. As a result, I'm calmer and I feel more in control of my emotions. I can look at life from a third person's point of view. This has also developed in me a sense of being non-judgemental and seeing people, things and situations for how they really are and not coloured by my emotions!

My personal biggest advantage and achievement now is that there is no sense of worry, anxiety or fear. Nothing to win or lose! My score now is a fantastic 10 most of the time. I truly want to thank Iggy for this technique. Certainly a life-changing one!!

Chapter 7

WHY HAPPINESS SWEEPING WORKS?

WHY IT WORKS

You are probably thinking that the improvements to the participants' happiness scores is all in their minds and perhaps it is not even real. That is the ultimate point. Happiness is in the mind and if you are happy in your mind, you are happy.

So how does happiness sweeping affect your mind? In my view, happiness sweeping is a process of acceptance without judgement, followed by letting go. By identifying a craving, fear or frustration in your inner mind, in a non-judgemental, gentle and loving way, you will achieve the first part, which is acceptance. Often we are shameful of even admitting that we have certain cravings and aversions. Yes, I acknowledge that I have *a craving for success*, it is okay and I am not ashamed of it. I acknowledge that I have a *fear of losing my job*, it is okay and I am not ashamed of it. This is a process of gentle embrace, pure acceptance and compassion to yourself.

Once you have identified the nature of yourself and the world as it is, you realise that you cannot change nor control it, thus you will begin to 'let go'. This is the process involving the throwing away hand action from happiness sweeping, which symbolises 'letting go'. The throwing away gesture and declaration that the craving/aversion 'is gone' helps it along its way out of your subconscious. It is as if you are saying, *"Yes, I acknowledge and embrace the craving/aversion, but it is now time to go."* Recently, I shared the happiness technique with a practising psychologist, Daryl Chow, MA, Ph.D. (Psych), who is an author of several research publications and books on mental health. Dr Chow noted the effectiveness of the visceral sweeping action as it took it away from the mind. His feedback was positive; saying that the technique is simple to do and the physical action of sweeping and throwing away reinforced the sense of letting go. He adds,*"I've tried other symbolic forms other than hand gesture-sweeping. (picking up cards and throwing it away, etc). I also used, "…and I let that go," instead of "it is gone…" I find this more proximal to a person's experience that to stretch a definite "it's gone." You see similarities in a couple of more recent approaches in therapy, like coherence approach, EMDR, EFT, etc"*.

Happiness sweeping works because it is letting go freely, without allowing the Ego self the chance to sabotage the process. There is no mental argument against the Ego self, which is the master generator of these cravings and aversions in the first place. Happiness sweeping has been shown to be able to quieten the inner mind chatter and bring about mindfulness without even trying to be mindful. It is as if you're standing in front of a loud talk-back radio; how can you be mindful when there is constant loud noise in your head? Telling someone to be mindful of their thoughts in this setting is impossible. We need to firstly turn the radio off and then within the quiet space, mindfulness will exist. Everything becomes clearer when there is no inner chatter.

Happiness sweeping creates emotional gratitude; a sense of wonder, thankfulness and appreciation for life. Happiness sweeping is a rapid mind therapy that you can do by yourself. It is simple, quick and easy, which with regular implementation will train your mind.

"The more man meditates upon good thoughts, the better will be his world and the world at large."

Confucius

YOUR BRAIN STRUCTURE CHANGES

There has been much research and discovery that the human brain has the ability to reorganise itself by forming new neural connections over the course of a human life time. This reorganisation is called neuroplasticity. Neuroplasticity allows the neurons (nerve cells) in the brain to compensate for injury and disease. Your brain structure changes in response to new situations or changes in the environment.

Dr Sara Lazar, a neuroscientist at Massachusetts General Hospital and Harvard Medical School, was one of the first scientists to make an anecdotal claim about the benefits of meditation and mindfulness. Through brain scans, she found that meditating can literally change your brain. Her studies found that long-term meditators had an increased amount of grey matter in the insula and sensory regions of the brain, as well as the auditory and sensory cortex. These areas of the brain are associated with peace, compassion memory and executive decision-making. I discuss Lazar's work in more detail in Chapter 9.

It is my belief that through happiness sweeping, the feelings of peace, joy and compassion that develops, begins to rewire the frontal cortex of our brain. This is the reason that with continual practice, it becomes easier and easier to be naturally at peace in the mind. This restructuring in the brain achieves long-term sustainable happiness in the mind.

TRYING TO BE POSITIVE ALL THE TIME DOESN'T WORK

Researchers from the positive psychology field of science talk about controlling the mind or thinking positively in order to maintain happiness. Unfortunately this is very difficult to achieve as the Ego self is essentially uncontrollable; it causes suffering and leads to unhappiness. Trying to change your thoughts with logical arguments and trying to force yourself to think positively all the time doesn't work. The mental debate or dissonance increases the chatter and noise in your mind, which is what disrupts your peace and happiness in the first place. The only thing you can do is acknowledge the negative thoughts, accept them without judgement and let them go. As you keep sweeping negative thoughts away, the empty space left behind gradually fills with peaceful and positive thoughts. It is a very different process than trying to force yourself to think positively most of the time.

CREATING INTENTIONS, NOT CRAVINGS

Are goals just cravings and do they create unhappiness? How can you have a life without goals? These are the two most important questions that I get asked a lot of the time. Yes, goals are cravings if you tie you happiness to the outcomes. If you somehow delay a little bit of happiness by waiting for a goal to be achieved then essentially you have created a craving. Cravings create dissatisfaction and unhappiness. People have expressed concern that the removal of their cravings might mean an end to their goals and subsequent motivation and achievements. They are fearful of being 10/10 happy and sitting under a tree for the rest of their life.

So can you create a goal without it being a craving? These are what I call 'intentions'; a casual, non-attached energy where your happiness is not tied to it. For example, if I had a craving for a job promotion and my happiness is tied to the realisation of this event; having this craving means I might have worries (of it taking too long) or fears (that it will never happen); perhaps frustrations (of not having the right skills), guilt (maybe in myself for not working hard enough) and anxiety (if I got the job, could I do it properly?). As you can see there is a whole bunch of possible mental anguish associated with a single craving for just one goal, a job promotion. Is it worth it?

On the other hand I could metaphorically create an 'intention' towards getting a promotion without attaching any cravings or aversions to it. This is the process of 'letting go' of the final outcome. So in this case, if I do get the promotion I am happy and if I don't get the promotion I am equally happy. I am not suffering by waiting for something to happen in order to satisfy my craving.

An intention:

"At some point, when I am ready or the time is right, I will be offered a job promotion"

Or

"I create a possibility that some day I will be promoted"

The distinction here is that not having a craving doesn't mean you do not pursue a job promotion. It just means that your happiness is not tied to the final outcome. The Zen saying that captures this distinction is, *"the key element to manifesting what you want is to let go of what you want"*. Remember the journey is more important than reaching the peak.

So, not having a craving for wealth doesn't mean that you have to give your money away or give up your job to stop earning money. It just means that you no longer desire it in the same worrying way and your happiness is not tied to it. When this happens your craving for extrinsic goals or outer happiness is reduced. By lessening your cravings and aversions for material and external things, it nourishes the Inner self and the intrinsic attainment of inner happiness.

10/10 HAPPINESS

Undoubtedly you have been sceptical about the ability of some people to reach 10/10 happiness, especially for the eight participants in the sweeping study. Cease judgement. Remember, it is their personal score in their mind and if they believe their happiness is a 10/10 then they are 10/10; people know their own happiness. You cannot fake a personal happiness score especially to yourself. What I found with these participants is that they all reported a complete state of peace, contentment, joy and bliss. The 10/10 participants will tell you that they no longer have cravings for wealth and material things in the same way as before. In fact, they hardly have any cravings or aversions at all. They no longer worry, stress or have anxiety. They are in a state of complete peace and happiness. Nothing makes them angry or frustrated any more. If something bothers them they sweep it away immediately and they have the tools to restore their happiness quickly. They no longer have any fears, including the fear of dying, getting sick or growing old. Their 'mental chatter' is quiet, to the point where there is complete clarity in the mind and their intuition is heightened. Their Ego self is tamed. They no longer concern themselves with the past or the future and they can all honestly say they are present and living in the now. They agree that they have achieved cessation of mental suffering and are living a life of complete contentment, joy and bliss; an enlightened state of being. The Hindu tradition describes this as an *'inner calmness, that quiet state of least excitation, even when we are dynamically busy'*. Can you describe yourself as being in this state?

WHAT'S HOLDING YOU BACK FROM 10/10?

Often people's happiness scores dramatically increase to 7, 8 or 9 out of 10 after the introduction of happiness sweeping. The question I ask them after regular practice is, "what is holding you back from reaching 10/10?" Are you waiting for something to happen in your life, like winning the lottery, achieving a perfect relationship, paying off your mortgage, going on a holiday, or for your children to leave home? Since we have already established that happiness is purely in the mind, there is nothing else external that you should be waiting for to be 10/10 happy. The only possible impediment to you feeling 10/10 is something hidden in your mind or at the depths of your subconscious, which might be holding you back. Here are some possible reasons why you might be stuck:

HIDDEN CRAVINGS AND AVERSIONS

One reason that you are not at 10/10 is that there are cravings and aversions still sitting deep down in your subconscious, yet to be identified and swept away. These hidden 'road blocks' are perhaps what's holding your happiness back. You have buried or suppressed the cravings and aversions deep enough that you don't even realise they're there. Throughout our lives we protect ourselves from all the years of suffering by burying the pain deep in our subconscious mind; sometimes for very long periods of time.

To find them, keep sweeping and the layers will peel away like an onion. The buried cravings and aversions will start to become easier to locate, identify and sweep. For example, I was working with John, a participant in the study who was sitting at a happiness level of 5, having improved from a 3/10. However, despite regular sweeping, John seemed to be stuck at 5. Then one day, just through reflection, it occurred to him that he had a fear of his wife who was mentally unstable and sometimes violent. It came like a lightning bolt from deep within his mind and when he started to sweep his fear of his wife away, his happiness shot up to 8/10 straight away.

I AM NOT WORTHY

Another possible reason for not being 10/10 happy is the subconscious mind judging you as being unworthy. Deep down you still think that your external life has to be perfect or problem-free before you ultimately let yourself be 10/10. Your subconscious mind is fearful that people will judge you as crazy if you have claimed perfect happiness when your life is clearly not perfect. People still judge happiness from the external environment.

GOALS REQUIRED FOR MOTIVATION

Your subconscious mind won't allow you to get to 10/10 in order to keep you keen and motivated. The fear of allowing you to be 10/10 is that you will no longer have aspirations for improvement. Like the fear that you will just spend the rest of your life sitting under a tree in blissful contentment. Your subconscious won't let that happen. Let me assure you that you will continue to strive and do great things at 10/10; the only difference is that you will achieve it without stress, worry and frustration.

IT IS JUST A BLIND SPOT

A blind spot is a craving or aversion that is staring at you in the face (not necessarily deep down) but you cannot see it. This usually involves close relationships with a bunch of highly emotionally-charged cravings and aversions. The blind spot is so obvious to others but it is very difficult for the participant to detect. If you find you may be stuck in the same situation; not moving your score, here are some questions that might help you visualise the blind spot.

- What thoughts still make you feel slightly sad?
- What thoughts still make you a little frustrated?
- What thoughts still make you feel anxious?
- What do you still want to happen but that hasn't yet?

HAPPINESS SWEEPING AND THE GRIEF PROCESS

Doctors have identified five common stages of grief, which includes denial, anger, bargaining, depression and acceptance. People experiencing grief take their own time to go through the stages; reaching the final stage of grief is when the person accepts the reality of their loss and that it can't be changed. Sometimes the grief process can last for months or even years. When you reach the acceptance stage, although you still feel sad, you're able to start moving forward with your life.

I would like to introduce you to Lesley who is a retired school teacher. She practises regular happiness sweeping and regular Twin Hearts meditation. Lesley's story appears at the end of Chapter 5. Lesley has a general happiness score of 10/10 most of the time. A few months ago, Lesley's elderly mother who lives with her passed away peacefully in her sleep. Her mother was well at the time, lively, even attending a wedding anniversary the night before. The passing was unexpected. As you would imagine, Lesley and her family were extremely shocked, saddened and devastated by their sudden loss. Lesley said that her happiness score plummeted to 3 on the morning she discovered her mother in bed. The pain of loss and profound sadness hit her hard. Lesley was very close to her mother; but felt glad that she went in peace, surrounded by those that loved her.

Lesley continued her regular practice of both sweeping and meditation and by day 6 (after her mother's passing), which was the day of the funeral, Lesley's inner happiness returned to around 7. On day 8, Lesley happiness score was back at around 10/10. Wow! Lesley demonstrated pure acceptance and letting go. I saw Lesley at the funeral and she looked so calm and peaceful. When you are 10/10 happy, it doesn't mean that you do not suffer when you are facing challenging events. Of course you will suffer because you are human, but you have the tools to recover quickly and restore your happiness. Being unhappy doesn't change the outcome of someone's passing. We have no control of death. Lesley even said she felt a little guilty that she recovered and re-established her happiness so quickly. How can you be happy when you just lost your mother?

In the case of Lesley, she felt some sense of acceptance in just over one week and no longer felt sadness as a result. Of course, she will always miss her mother, but Lesley is a shining example of how the practice of happiness sweeping protects one's inner happiness. Some of you might believe that Lesley should at least be in mourning for the next few months to honour her late mother. I am sure her mother wouldn't want that for Lesley or her family. Yet your Ego self has a view of how much we should suffer. Fortunately, when you are 10/10 happy like Lesley, you have the tools to recover quickly rather than remaining painfully sad or depressed.

YOU STILL HAVE TO FETCH WATER

It is important to understand that just because you are 10/10 happy and maybe enlightened, you still have to deal with the challenges of being a human being.

> Before enlightenment, fetch water.
> After enlightenment, fetch water.
> — Buddhist proverb

You still have to pay your bills; you still have to deal with badly-behaved teenagers; politics within the workplace; and still have to come home to a nagging spouse; all the while living in a world gone crazy, with environmental degradation, endless violence and so on. These are all external things that don't change. Life goes on.

At least with happiness sweeping you have a tool to help you recover from the challenges that life throws at you, no matter how bad. You will still have to fetch water or you will die of thirst. The difference with being enlightened or 10/10 happy is that your internal environment is constant.

You have achieved the cessation of suffering and are living a life of complete peace, contentment, joy and bliss; an enlightened state of being – **but you still have to fetch water.**

Answers to your questions...

Q. Do I really have to 'let go' as I sweep?

A. Yes the whole idea is to 'let go' but it is always difficult to let go of cravings and aversions that you have held and nurtured for many years. My advice is to just start by going through the verbal and physical sweeping steps and keep practicing daily. Eventually you will get to a point where you can finally, fully let go. It is like peeling an onion, the outer layers are more difficult to peel initially; but it gets easier with more reflection and sweeping.

Q. Why is sweeping a counter-intuitive process?

A. Most people who have tried it have had trouble trying to understand how the sweeping process actually works. It is counter-intuitive. For example, how can I let go of the craving for my friend to get well from cancer when I do actually want him to get well? The point is that mental suffering about your friend's cancer is not going change the outcome, whatever it is. Letting go is just relieving your worry and mental suffering. It is counter-intuitive that, in order to manifest what you want, you actually have to let go of what you want. It doesn't make much sense and that's why 10/10 happiness is so elusive. I usually tell people to stop thinking about how it works and just do the exercise without judgement or analysis.

Q. Can you be 10/10 happy whilst imprisoned?

A. I often pose this hypothetical question to participants. Some say no; they couldn't envisage being happy in a prison cell. Others say in theory yes, but it would be very difficult to achieve. Once again, happiness is in the mind and if one can be happy in the mind, then the external state has no influence. So in theory, if a prisoner can sweep away cravings, such as to be out of prison, to see their family; cravings for better conditions or better food; cravings for a shorter sentence etc; then they could achieve 10/10 happiness. If a prisoner could sweep away fears of never getting out; fear of loneliness or isolation, then the prisoner would be on the way to pure 10/10 happiness. Pure acceptance of the imprisonment.

Claire's Story...

The positive outcomes from the sweeping technique have been enormous for my mental health. As a 47 year-old I started to notice changes within my life. I was becoming less tolerant to external factors that were affecting me. I was struggling with work, university study and personal life balance.

I was introduced to Twin Hearts meditation through a work friend. I noticed immediate positive results in my outlook on life; issues that once bothered me were no longer issues anymore. After a few months of regular meditation sessions I was introduced to 'Happiness Sweeping' by Iggy Tan.

In the beginning my happiness score was a 5/10. Iggy introduced our group to regular 'Sweeping' techniques. We needed to categorise our wants and desires as well as our fears and frustrations. The challenges I found was how to articulate my thoughts into words and how to verbalise what was really bothering me. After some time regularly daily sweeping, sometimes twice daily, my thoughts and emotions started to flow; and, like peeling an onion each layer of emotion would uncover new thoughts and emotions until I hit the core problem. This deep issue was the desire to be liked and to be thought of as intelligent. A perfect example of this is my worry of whether people at work or my university friends thought that I was smart enough.

I would project this anxiety that resulted in a craving with an impulse for buying high-end expensive shoes. I later realised that what I was doing was filling a void with a craving and a need. If I bought expensive shoes I realised that all my colleagues would comment on how lovely the shoes were. This would start a discussion that would make me feel liked by the group of women.

The initial results of the sweeping technique were instant relief; the habit I developed was to sweep in the shower allowing all the dirty, negative energy to run down the drain. As a beginner I would recommend setting aside some time in the morning and/or evening; maybe write a note on the fridge to remind you to sweep daily. My biggest piece of advice would be to team the sweeping technique with some meditation even if meditation is only performed once a week.

The benefits I have noticed, as well as my friends, are that my emotions are not so bottled up and that my life just flows smoothly. In regards to my mental health I feel that my thoughts are more organised. The best way to describe me before happiness sweeping was like a car running out of petrol - with a stop/start motion - and now life is so much smoother. My current happiness score is an amazing 10/10. Happy sweeping!

Chapter 8

TAMING THE EGO SELF

EGO SELF

'Ego' is a word defined by the Oxford Dictionary as *"the part of the mind that mediates between the conscious and the unconscious; and the part of the mind responsible for reality testing and a sense of personal identity"*. 'Ego self' is a person's sense of self; a person's Ego develops from his or her experiences throughout life. The Ego self is defined by external factors such as social forces, experiences and relationships.

Unfortunately the Ego self we develop as children never maps to reality when we're adults. For example, *"I'm not good at school"; "My freckles make me ugly"; "Nobody likes me"; "I am better than her."* Problems arise when the Ego self is negative, inaccurate or even overly positive. Our Ego self plays an immense role in creating emotional chaos in our lives. This chaos creates suffering and adversely affects our happiness. The pursuit of material things, success, image and external goals sits within the Ego self. As the master generator of cravings and aversions, the Ego self can cause a lot of suffering and unhappiness.

INNER SELF

The Inner self, on the other hand, is a person's true or inner soul. The Oxford Dictionary defines the Inner self as "a person's true or internal mind, soul, or nature". Some believe the Inner self is well developed, pure and perfect at birth. The Inner self is a state of consciousness that can be accessed through meditation and introspection, which promotes greater self-awareness and acceptance. I believe that true happiness, peace, contentment, joy and bliss sits within the Inner self.

YOU ARE THE RING MASTER

Throughout the book I reinforce the idea that the number one obstacle for allowing yourself to be truly happy is your Ego self. Whilst I may often sound overly negative towards the Ego self, we still actually need it. We need our sense of self and the drive, motivation and energy that the Ego self provides. Unfortunately we have allowed the Ego self to take control and run the show. It is now time to start nourishing the Inner self and restore the balance. Let's explore how we can tame our Ego selves while nourishing our Inner selves.

BATTLE OF THE SUPERHEROES

Firstly, I'll tell you a story about two superhero arch rivals: one is the Ego self and the other is the Inner self. Both have been battling to win control of the show – you. These two superheroes, the Ego self superhero (ESS) and the Inner self superhero (ISS) have existed from the day you were born and have been in battle ever since. As a baby, the ISS was strong and prominent. It had joy and bliss as super powers, which was your state of being as a baby. On the other hand, the ESS was only minor in the early days, but it began to develop quickly and strongly as you grew. Unfortunately, the ESS is much smarter and more cunning than the ISS and so it soon realised that it could win control of the show by controlling the thoughts in your mind. By controlling your thoughts, the ESS could ultimately control you.

Ego Self   Inner Self

So the ESS propaganda commenced and from then on your young adult mind has been filled with unrelenting chatter under ESS control. *"I want to be successful to be happy; I want to be rich to be happy; I want to be attractive to be happy; I want people to like me to be happy; I am not good enough; I am a fake; people don't like me"* and on and on it goes. The ESS has become very strong over the years and is now the dominant force in your adult life. The ESS doesn't care about peace and happiness. The ISS, who is the provider of peace, contentment, joy and bliss, is now too diminished and weakened to be able to have any influence over the ESS. This is the battle of the superheroes to win control of your mind.

LESS EGO, MORE OTHERS (LEMO)

I will now offer some tips for you to try to tame your Ego self. These tips all relate some way or another to the mind and the way it operates. Constantly thinking about how to make things better for yourself is exhausting, stressful and ultimately leads to unhappiness. It's time to stop being preoccupied with yourself, fuelled by your Ego self. Instead focus more on others, less on yourself and turn *on* a switch in your mind, which I call the 'less Ego, more others' or LEMO switch. Turning the LEMO switch on in the mind tames the Ego self and enables feelings of happiness and contentment.

Turning on the LEMO switch directs power and relevance to your Inner self where happiness sits. Work on making other people happy, not yourself. If meeting the bills is going to be tight, give a small donation to a charity regardless. If time is important to you, donate your time to helping others and the community. Help someone in need. These are ways you can turn the LEMO switch *on* in your mind.

Extensive research has shown that kindness and focus on others improves your inner happiness. The LEMO switch being activated often relieves guilt, distress or discomfort over others' difficulties and sufferings, and encourages a sense of awareness and appreciation for your own good fortune. Some of us turn the switch *on* and *off* at different periods of time, whilst others have the LEMO switched on permanently all the time.

PRACTICE LOVING KINDNESS AND COMPASSION

The practice of loving kindness and compassion (will turn on the LEMO switch) can sound a bit 'new age' or over the top but is essentially core to most religions. This core message of love characterised by acts of kindness, generosity and gentleness is what all religions of today are essentially based on. The practice is not only worthwhile for society as a whole to adopt but particularly worthwhile for the individual as it improves happiness and mental well-being. Since this book is about happiness and not other topics (religion), let's focus on the benefits of practicing loving kindness and compassion in relation to one's inner peace and happiness.

Try to consider how you might feel after helping a stranger? This is of course without the expectation of receiving anything in return from the stranger. How would you feel after showing an act of kindness to someone you did not know? Like showing compassion by donating money, food or volunteering your time? It has been proven, through extensive research, that such altruistic and philanthropic acts as just mentioned generate an improvement in one's inner happiness; the LEMO switch is activated. When you volunteer to help your local community or give to a homeless person in need, how do you feel? As stated in an article published in the Journal of Social Psychology (2012), discussing a research study on kindness and happiness, it's not only happier people who are kinder, but also kinder people who are happier.

Michael Norton, Assistant Professor from the Harvard Business School, conducted a series of studies with his colleagues at the University of British Columbia. Together they demonstrated that people are happier when they spend money on others as opposed to themselves. The work included a USA nation-wide survey in which the researchers interviewed a total of 632 people, both men and women; the questions asked the participants how much they earned annually; how much they spent each month on bills, expenses and gifts for themselves; and what they spent monthly on gifts for other people and donations to charities. They also asked them to rate their level of happiness. The findings showed that those who reported spending more on others, what the team called 'prosocial' spending, also reported a greater level of happiness, while the money expended on themselves had no impact on the person's happiness.

In another experiment, the same group of researchers handed out envelopes of money to students on a university campus. The recipients were asked to spend the money (either with five dollars or $20 in the envelope) by the end of that day. The money was to be spent on themselves, or to be spent on someone else or donating it to a charity. The results of the experiment mirrored the results from the aforementioned study, *"We found that people who spent the money on themselves that day weren't happier that evening,"* the Harvard Business School professor said. *"But those recipients who spent it on others were happier. The amount of money, five dollars or $20, didn't matter at all. It was only how people spent it that made them happier."* Once again, the LEMO switch was turned *on* by these study participants who spent the money on others.

A high profile example of LEMO is the Giving Pledge created by Bill and Melinda Gates and Warren Buffett. The goal of the Giving Pledge organisation is to inspire wealthy people to give at least half of their net worth to humanity, either during their lifetime or upon their death. This was inspired by the example set by millions of people around the world from all income levels who give generously and often at great personal sacrifice to make the world better. The act of giving makes people happier. As of 2017 the Giving Pledge had a total of 158 signers, either as individuals or couples; some of whom have since died. Most of the signers of the pledge are or were billionaires; their pledges combined total over $365 billion. In my opinion, the act of pledging turns the LEMO switch *on* in a donor's mind; it severs the emotional attachment to money and develops a deep sense of happiness.

STARTS WITH THE MIND AND THOUGHTS

How do I practise loving kindness and compassion? Is it just physical acts of kindness? Or is it the thoughts in my mind as well as my speech? If you believe that thought is energy and is also the key to creating your reality, then you will understand that practicing loving kindness and compassion starts in the mind. Mahatma Gandhi said *"A man is but the product of his thoughts. What he thinks, he becomes"*.

So, if you think sad and angry thoughts you will feel sad, angry and the negative energy will thus perpetuate. In order to live as a kind and compassionate person, you need to think loving kindness and compassionate thoughts. I believe that your speech and actions will then follow and will align once you have these thoughts. Turn the LEMO switch *on* in your head and everything will follow. That's why loving kindness and compassionate meditation is effective as it creates these thoughts which in turn creates your reality. Peaceful and compassionate thoughts improves your inner happiness. Gandhi refers to this by summarising, *"Happiness is when what you think, what you say and what you do are in harmony"*.

The next challenge is how to control your thoughts so they are centred on loving kindness and compassion. Luckily, this is made easy due to the regular happiness sweeping and blessing of enemies helping you to practise loving kindness and compassion in your mind. Choose to be kind and compassionate by monitoring your thoughts, speech and then your actions. Once you become aware of this internal criteria, you will become aware of every thought, word or action and whether it matches the criteria. I sometimes catch myself with a thought and realise that it is full of judgement and prejudice, turning the LEMO switch *off*. Sweeping helps turn the LEMO switch back *on* as explained in this next example.

Example: "I think Jack is an idiot; he is really affecting my happiness."

Sweeping: *"My craving for Jack to be how I want him to be is gone. My craving for Jack to understand my position is gone. My craving to judge Jack is gone. My craving to change Jack is gone. My frustration for Jack's incompetence is gone. My frustration for Jack's unacceptable behaviour is gone."*

Blessing: (Raise your hands), *"I bless and wish Jack with peace, lots of prosperity, abundance and every success in the world. I bless and wish him with happiness and contentment. I bless him and his family with joy and good health."* (My LEMO switch is activated).

From the above sweeping and blessing example, I managed to shift my emotional state from being very upset and angry with Jack to a state of peace and compassion. The sweeping removes the negative energy and the blessing replaces it with positive peaceful energy. Blessing an enemy or someone that upsets you is like practicing forgiveness but in a very powerful proactive way.

If you have an unkind thought about someone then you are not practicing loving kindness and compassion (so sweep it away). If you are saying unkind things about someone, which derived from the unkind thought, then you are not practicing loving kindness and compassion (so sweep it away). If you are doing something unpleasant to someone , which derived from an unkind thought, then you are not practicing loving kindness and compassion (sweep it away). It all starts from the unkind thoughts (mental chatter) in the first place.

"This is my simple religion. There is no need for temples; no need for complicated philosophy. Our own brain, our own heart is our temple; the philosophy is kindness"

Dalai Lama

EXPECTATION IS THE PROBLEM

There is a slight glitch with the LEMO switch though; it won't stay switched *on* if there is any expectation of a return or a reward involved. As shown in the previous research, kindness and focus on others creates inner happiness for the giver. Let's examine what happens when we throw 'expectation' (driven by the Ego self) into the mix. Imagine you're walking past a homeless person in the street and you stop to give five dollars to this person. After giving the money you feel good as you continue walking by believing you have just helped someone in need. Now imagine the same scenario but instead add an expectation that you will at least receive some form of gratitude; a 'thank you' from the receiver. However, no response is given at all. In this scenario you might feel disappointed, annoyed or even slightly regretful, because there was no sign of expected appreciation to your kindness. The Ego self is hurt and angry. So the same act of kindness for both scenarios can create such different happiness outcomes if you add 'expectation' to your mindset.

So if you are practicing loving kindness and compassion by giving with the expectation of something in return, there is a chance that you might negate the process of developing inner happiness and peace. The LEMO switch in the mind will not stay *on*. Expectation for something in return might be as simple as an acknowledgement, praise, an offer of a returned favour, business contacts, friendship, monetary reward, improved status, image or even a simple 'thank you'. Giving is better done with little or no expectation for anything back. Expectation in relationships is the biggest source of discontentment; but more on this later in the chapter.

MY TAKE ON KARMA

We often misinterpret the concept of Karma as giving to others on the proviso that something good will come back in return. Karma is defined as a spiritual principle of cause and effect where intent and actions of an individual (cause) influence the future of that individual (effect). Most of us assume that giving will result in something good for us in the future like material gains, a new car or house or good fortune like winning lottery. Karma is typically viewed as a punishment tool for those who we believe have misbehaved towards us. My simple interpretation of Karma is that good intentions and good deeds make you happy. Bad or unkind intentions and deeds increases the turbulence and suffering in your mind. There is no material gain from practicing loving kindness and compassion, just inner happiness and peace. I call this 'instant karma' or 'instant gain'; worth more than any material gain. The message here is simple: to help you along the path to 10/10 happiness, practise loving kindness and compassion (without expectation) to others and importantly, to yourself.

THE RIGHT VIEW IS A 'NON-JUDGEMENTAL' VIEW

Maintaining the 'right view' is to not have a 'judgemental view' or a view that is free of judgement. Judgement originates from cravings and aversions in the mind. The Ego self is the master of judgement and blame. Judgement keeps the LEMO switch *off*, creating frustration and intolerance that leads to suffering and unhappiness. Having a judgemental view is a craving or aversion – sweep it away! Instead a 'neutral view' or 'no view' allows you to be open and accepting; enriching the flow of loving kindness and compassion.

If I had a view that unemployed people are lazy then this judgemental view prevents me from thinking of any unemployed person in a positive light. I am not likely to treat these people with kindness and compassion. I am not likely to want to offer any help to someone looking for a job because of this prejudice. Remember, the practice of loving kindness and compassion starts in the mind first. To alter this view I need to constantly sweep the associated cravings and aversions about the unemployed and a neutral view about them will eventually develop. To help us maintain the right view (or a neutral view), remember the philosophy that there is no right or wrong, there's no good or bad. It is what it is.

WHAT ARE YOU LOOKING FORWARD TO?

Now, try to spend a few moments to think about something that you are currently looking forward to. It might be an upcoming holiday, birthday, promotion or a celebration. You might look forward to completing a project you've been working on; or your friend's wedding. Someone asked me recently if I was looking forward to a holiday that I had coming up; I thought about it and I could honestly say I was completely neutral about it. Looking forward to something implies that the moment in the future is going to be better than the moment today. Is that because the external conditions are going to be more pleasant and hence you will be happier? I feel 10/10 today so how could I feel any happier next week on my holiday. I am happy and contented today and I will be equally happy and contented while on my upcoming holiday. I would say that this is living in the present moment.

> Man, he is so anxious about the future that he does not enjoy the present; the result being that he does not live in the present or the future; he lives as if he is never going to die and then dies having never really lived.
>
> Dalai Lama

TAKING 100% RESPONSIBILITY

Now let's examine the Ego self in personal relationships. One of the hardest challenges in our lifetime is establishing, developing and maintaining a loving connection with a partner. The highs are great but the lows are sometimes unbearable. We learn that for better or for worse a partnership or marriage is all about compromise. Let's face it, compromise means each partner making concessions. In order to make concessions we are continually evaluating what we put into the relationship and what we get out of it. The ultimate fair deal would be one side putting 50 percent of effort into the relationship and the other side satisfied that they are getting 50 percent back in return. If each partner was satisfied (exactly 50/50) then I guess we have a good compromise and the relationship is fair.

Unfortunately, relationships don't always work that way. Here comes that dreaded word again, 'expectation'; the root of all unhappiness. The problem with most relationships is that our Ego self has a personal biased opinion that we (or I) put more into the relationship than our partner, we feel as though we receive less benefits compared to our partner. For example, *"I give 60 percent and only get back 40 percent from the partnership"*. It is never 50/50 in each partner's mental scoreboard. In the past I would often think to myself that I am right and my wife is the one who has to change, not me. How could she not see it my way, I would ask myself? I have to convince and make her understand that I am right and she is wrong; the mental chatter ensues!

Put simply, we rely on our partners to make us happy and satisfy our emotional and physical needs. We expect to receive love in certain ways. When they don't deliver what we expect or if they refuse to change to fit our expectations, we become unhappy and discontented. What happened to the idea that happiness is in your mind - and only in your mind? Forget about trying to change your partner and focus on changing your mindset.

So let's suspend judgement for a moment and try to imagine that you have re-trained your Ego self to allow you to give 100 percent to your relationship while expecting nothing or zero percent in return. Yes, zero return. Your LEMO switch is firmly *on*. This is along the same lines as unconditional love; like the love for your own baby. The pure act of giving this love to your partner and declaring the responsibility is in itself satisfying; it brings about happiness as it is without any expectation for anything in return.

About 15 years ago, after completing a self-development course, I came home to my wife and declared to her that I was going to take 100 percent responsibility of making our relationship great without any expectation from her. My wife thought I was *loopy* at the time but over the years until this day, I try to act with this state of mind. I agree that this declaration is not easy to achieve; and it is certainly difficult to maintain; but we must constantly wrestle our Ego self to tame it. If one partner needs to take responsibility and apologise if things are not going well, I generally do so without expecting any responsibility from my wife. If some action needs to be taken to keep the relationship on track then I will do it without expectation. In my mind, I am the only person that has the power or mandate to make or keep the relationship great. If my wife contributes like she usually does, it is absolutely not expected or required but appreciated, all the same. The key here is taming expectation, thus the Ego self. Is it hard to do and maintain? Yes, absolutely; your first reaction is always to seek blame or control of your partner and then fairness and justice comes into play. You have to remind yourself of the 100 percent declaration, swallow your Ego pride and take full responsibility for making the relationship great once again.

By now you are undoubtedly thinking I must be a pushover. I can't stand up for myself and I am in a position of weakness all the time. Let me reassure you – if you can achieve this state of being you are actually in a very powerful position. You are no longer a slave of the Ego self. What is likely to happen if you are the first to say sorry; the first to take responsibility; the first to implement a corrective action; the first to accept blame; the first to initiate a discussion or the first to resolve a relationship issue? The likely outcome is that you have a great and fulfilling relationship. The act of giving (less Ego, more others) provides you with inner peace, contentment and as such, a loving, harmonious relationship. The unintentional outcome of simply loving your partner more deeply is that you are loved more deeply.

My friend says (in jest) that the only reason I can take 100 percent responsibility for my marriage is that I am married to a saint. But in reality all relationships require constant effort and nurturing, even with a saint for a partner. Another interesting point is that you can't fake the responsibility declaration to your partner unless you are totally 100 percent aligned in mind and soul.

"We come to love not by finding a perfect person, but by learning to see an imperfect person perfect"

Sam Keen

I was recently explaining the 100 percent responsibility concept to another friend, who responded, *"What a great idea, can you please tell my husband about it?"*; as you can see my dear friend missed the point completely. Happiness and contentment come from inside your mind, not from someone else trying to make you feel happy. When you turn the LEMO switch *on* in your mind, happiness flows; it is as simple as that.

At some stage along your happiness journey you may be at the point where your Ego self is sufficiently tamed and you are feeling self-actualised. I would say at this point you're ready to make the 100 percent responsibility declaration to your partner.

The Declaration:
"From now on, I take 100 percent responsibility for making our relationship great, without any expectation from you".

Answers to your questions…

Q. Has anyone ever reached 10/10 from one single happiness sweeping session?

A. I demonstrated the sweeping technique to a participant who was siting at a happiness level of 6/10. As a single parent with four children and a partner dealing with cancer, she was very open and enthusiastic to try the technique. A lot of deep cravings and aversions started to be swept away and she was quite teary and emotional at times. After the session, I asked her if she felt lighter but she wasn't sure due to the emotions she was feeling after sweeping away a lot of stuff. We talked for about 15 minutes, and then I asked her what her happiness score was at that point. She blurted out '10/10' and was absolutely beaming. This was the first time I had witnessed someone hit 10/10 from one single session. The power of this technique still amazes me.

Q. Have you ever encountered a 10/10 happy person who has not practised happiness sweeping and/or meditation?

A. Recently, I met a business associate from Austria. During the conversation I asked him what his happiness score was and he said that he was 10/10. I had to clarify his answer by asking questions about worry, contentment, cravings, fears; after doing so I confirmed that he was indeed 10/10. I asked him if he meditated or had some way to remain in this state and he said he didn't. He said it started about 4 years ago. He somehow achieved the pure acceptance and letting go process all by himself. This was the first time I have met someone that is 10/10 without using the happiness sweeping technique or meditation. So once you face the acceptance and letting go process, remember that 10/10 happiness is very real and very possible to anyone.

Q. Why do I often wake in the morning with some anxiety?

A. Some of those who are at 8, 9, or even 10 on their happiness score have often asked me why they're happy throughout the day but initially wake up in the morning slightly stressed or anxious. They are puzzled and cannot explain why they feel that way when they are generally very happy otherwise. Throughout the day we are constantly aware of our happiness and we sweep to make sure no incoming cravings or aversions gets into our subconscious. We are in fact screening our thoughts and then sweeping if required. In the morning, when you are still asleep, you are dreaming of cravings and aversions as thoughts. Cravings, worries or fears are coming into your mind without a filter for removal. You're unaware of them as you are asleep and dreaming. These thoughts build-up, which causes the feeling of built-up stress and anxiety as you wake up. The only way to deal with them is to commence sweeping straight away as you wake up and are still lying in bed. This will quickly clear the cravings and aversions that have built-up overnight and will quickly restore your peace and happiness.

Carol's Story...

Happiness. A pretty big word and something we all feel moments of, hours of, days of and weeks. Sometimes there are many sad moments, which eat away at our happiness. Iggy's sweeping has helped me get back to most days feeling 10/10 happy.

My name is Carol and I am turning 50 next year. My happiness hasn't always been at about a seven. It plummeted to a very low 2-3. I had depression, the cause of which I can only put down to 'empty nesting'. Self-diagnosed later only when I was finding a way out. My daughter moved to Perth for school to follow a sporting desire in basketball through a scholarship. Then my son wanted to board closer to his school rather than sit on a bus every day. They were both going to be happier doing what they wanted to do and needed to do. But that left me empty... I really just wanted them to be happy. I don't think my husband understood my emotional breakdowns, tears and rants. I didn't either, even scared my children at times. Probably took me a year and I was still not aware that I had depression. Then I got a very energetic golden retriever that gave me a reason to get up before work and to walk. He gave me unconditional love and company. I was feeling happier, but still missed the kids being around.

This took quite a while to accept that they were growing up and I no longer had full control over them. It's possible my happiness has always been on hold as I like to make everyone happy. My parents, my friends, my husband, my children, in no particular order, just whoever needs it.

I have no control over my parents, they're adults right? They have been here a lot longer than me. I just wanted to try and get them to be healthier in their old age. Stop them drinking as much, smoke less, preferably not at all. I was letting it consume me, but then realised I am not in control of their happiness nor their lives; they are living it out the way they want to. As a massage and beauty therapist, I deal with a lot of people every day; some have amazing energy and others just zap you dry of good energy. Iggy's sweeping technique has helped me give people a few tips on becoming more positive by finding some happy place in their day to help get rid of the negative energy.

So with sweeping I have come to find that I have no control over other people's happiness, only my own. So when I started to rid my thoughts of things that stagnated me, made me feel negative and sad, I started to feel much clearer, happier and able to feel much better about myself. This reflected on my whole family. I am a big visualisation person. I lost that for years, but it's coming back, because my ability to get rid of the crap in my life is so much better with the sweeping out of the cravings.

I definitely believe there is a great reward in Iggy's happiness sweeping. I did feel like I was back at the confessional in church, letting Iggy in on my desires, cravings, failings, loss of control and aversions. Things just flowed once I started. You only have to do the technique once with Iggy and away you go. You can adapt it to wherever and whenever you feel the need. I do it when I am walking, usually in a place of serenity and beauty along the beach. A really good place to let go of the cravings and receive positive energy is from the ocean. My happiness level is 10/10 and I am living a life of complete peace, joy and bliss. Thank you Iggy for always being there to check on my happiness level and for being a wonderful friend.

Chapter 9

MEDITATION & MINDFULNESS

USE OF MEDITATION

The happiness sweeping technique I share in this book is essentially a mindfulness or meditative exercise. The sweeping process helps you bring your attention to the present moment. It brings awareness to the many cravings and aversions that are swirling around in your conscious and subconscious mind. Happiness sweeping is the easiest, quickest and most powerful technique to improve your happiness and peacefulness. However, if you want to boost your peace of mind and overall happiness, meditation combined with sweeping is also worth considering.

If you stop to just think about the number of thoughts that go through your mind every day, you'd probably guess hundreds and thousands of thoughts, all day, every day. These thoughts stem from the Ego self that creates non-stop, exhausting 'chatter' in the mind. Perhaps the fast-paced world we live in has something to do with it, but it seems like we all struggle to slow our minds down regardless.

The amazing part of meditation is that you are in a thoughtless state, which means much peace without thought. In this state, you will enjoy the present and with regular practise, your worries about the past and future will fade away. You will develop inner peace and unbelievable clarity of the mind.

WHAT IS MEDITATION?

Meditation is the psychological process of bringing attention to the internal experiences that occur in the present moment. The history of meditation dates back to thousands of years ago. Meditation is defined as a practice of concentrated focus on a sound, a breath, an object, some inner visualisation, movement, or attention itself in order to increase awareness of the present moment. Meditation can help with stress reduction, promoting relaxation or enhancing personal and spiritual growth.

WHAT IS MINDFULNESS?

The terms 'meditation' and 'mindfulness' are thrown around a lot these days and are often used interchangeably. Mindfulness is just one form of the many types of meditation. Both meanings tend to refer to the same idea, which is the calming of a frenzied mind. Mindfulness is the act of focusing on being in the present, such as focusing exclusively on a single, trivial task like drinking a cup of tea; this would require consideration to the scent of the tea, its warmth, it's taste and by doing so removing overpowering emotions from the mind. Psychologists have observed through 'mindfulness practice' research that some mental and physical conditions in patients can improve. An example is the way mindfulness practice promoted the reduction of depression-related symptoms in patients.

OBJECTIVES OF MEDITATION

Meditation is recognised today as an approach to training the mind. One of the objectives of meditation is to reach a deep state of relaxation, to calm emotions, still the mind and experience an expansion of consciousness. There are many types and forms of meditation that come from different traditions and cultures. Some of the more popular meditations today include Transcendental Meditation, Heart Rhythm Meditation, Kundalini, Guided Visualisation, Qi Gong, Zazen and Mindfulness.

THE SCIENCE OF MEDITATION

There is certainly an abundance of scientific research available to support the notion that meditation can reduce stress or increase happiness levels. Equally with the advent of breakthrough brain-scanning technologies, many researchers in the field have documented the changes in our brain structure (neuroplasticity) using meditation practitioners. As mentioned previously, Dr Sara Lazar, a neuroscientist at Massachusetts General Hospital and Harvard Medical School, was one of the first scientists to study the benefits of meditation and mindfulness. Through brain scans, she surprisingly found that meditating can literally change your brain.

Dr Lazar's first study in 2005 looked at long-term meditators versus a control group, which found that the long-term meditators had an increased amount of grey matter in the insula and sensory regions of the brain as well as the auditory and sensory cortex. According to Lazar, when you are mindful, you're paying attention to your breathing, to sounds, to the present moment and in turn shutting cognition down. Your senses are enhanced. Dr Lazar also found increased grey matter in the meditators' frontal cortex (front of brain), which is associated with memory and executive decision-making. Interestingly the brains of meditators aged over 50 contained the same amount of grey matter as those meditators aged under 25.

In a separate study, Dr Lazar also examined a group of people who had never meditated before. Some of the beginners participated in an eight-week mindfulness-based stress reduction program. Similarly, she found differences in brain volume in just eight weeks in five different regions in the brain. Besides reporting increased calmness, less stress and more peace, the group that meditate for eight weeks were found to have positive changes in their brain structures.

Dr Lazar's research demonstrates that the deep state of relaxation and calmness through meditation changes the brain structure for the betters. Other studies published in the same field have similarly concluded positive correlations between meditation and health. Meditation has been proven to be as effective in treating some forms of anxiety and depression as other treatments. The production of neurotransmitters such as serotonin, oxytocin and dopamine during meditation also promotes happiness.

There is a good reason that meditation practice, in all forms, has been around for over 2,500 years. It is only recently that modern medicine and science has developed techniques to measure the benefits of these ancient meditational practices.

MEDITATION ON TWIN HEARTS

My initial experience with meditation was challenging as I found my mind wandering off from constant inner chatter. Several years ago, Leena, a friend of mine, invited me to a 'Meditation on Twin Hearts' group. The meditation is guided and developed by Master Choa Kok Sui. The Twin Hearts meditation is practised by thousands of people from different religions, cultures and philosophies around the world.

Dr Glenn Mendoza, who I mentioned in Chapter 1, is also a practitioner of the Twin Hearts meditation. Mendoza studied the effects of this meditation; his research showed a decreased heart rate and respiratory rate by 15-20 percent, significant muscle relaxation measured by electromyogram and positive skin conductance. Mendoza's studies on brain waves showed an increased alpha, theta and delta; and notably, brain synchronisation. Brain synchronisation occurs when the right and left sides of the brain work in concert with each other, resonating at the same frequencies and causing neural pathways to fire rapidly and efficiently. He also conducted a follow-up study that looked into the relationship between meditation and neurohormones and neuropeptides. Increased serum levels (up to 300 percent) of melatonin (corrects sleep/wake patterns and prevents aging) were noted after the meditation sessions. Both studies were presented at international conventions.

Other Twin Hearts meditation studies (Mendoza's colleagues Jeff Tarrant and Neus Raines) used experienced meditators and non-meditators to test the meditation's effects. Subjectively, all participants of these studies showed increased happiness, emerging positive emotions and decreased levels of anxiety after meditation.

Gamma brain waves, which are associated with the 'feeling of blessings', peak concentration and extremely high levels of cognitive functioning, were noted to increase in the experienced meditators. Increased gamma waves are typically observed in experienced meditators such as monks and nuns.

When you begin a meditation practice it is important to let go of trying to do it perfectly. There is no perfect or right way. It is just a journey and you can't possibly mess it up. Find a type of meditation that suits you and your lifestyle. Just begin and see how meditation can benefit your mind, body and soul.

Answers to your questions...

Q. For how long do you have to meditate daily?

A. A common view held by experienced meditators is that any amount of meditation is better than none. The general recommendation is to start with five or ten minutes daily. Studies show that to get much higher activation of parts of the brain associated with feelings of well-being, at least 20 minutes of meditation a day is sufficient.

Q. I have trouble getting my mind to focus, what do I do?

A. I previously had the same problem from a busy and hectic mind. It was frustrating as my mind kept wandering off all the time during meditation. As I mentioned before I found the Twin Hearts meditation extremely effective because it was a guided meditation and we focused on projecting peace, love and compassion to the world and others (it can be accessed from the iTunes store if interested). If you want to meditate, find a meditation that works for you and that suits your lifestyle.

John's Story...

I am a 66 year-old man who has been married for some 40 years. I have much to be grateful for but could never really work out why I did not feel better about myself for my lucky life. I am currently suffering from Multiple Sclerosis, which has adversely affected my mobility and function. My partner is suffering from worsening physiological problems and she has been in and out of mental institutions. I am fearful of her as she can be violent and with my deteriorating Multiple Sclerosis condition, I am unable to defend myself. Unfortunately, I have come to realise that I have been subjected to various forms of emotional blackmail and bullying in my own home for many years.

I first met Iggy at meditation practice. During one of his happiness sessions, Iggy asked me what my level of happiness was out of ten. Almost instantly I came up with the number of 3; no idea where it came from but each time I asked myself the same question I again came up with the same answer. I guess at 3/10 I was unhappy.

I started regular happiness sweeping and I think I came up to 5 but nothing significant. This went on for about three weeks; then one night I was thinking about what my meditation leader had said. He had previously said that my partner's negative energy was adversely affecting me and I recalled that a naturopath had once said something very similar to me also. I didn't realise that I was being subjected to emotional blackmail by my wife. As a result I started to sweep the cravings and aversions around this emotional abuse and my happiness improved dramatically.

The next time I saw Iggy at meditation I was able to tell him I was sitting at 7 most of the time. My relationship with my wife, as you would imagine, is very difficult, stressful and has caused me a great deal of angst. She is mentally unstable. We have now separated and I have changed all the locks to my house for fear of her violent and erratic behaviour. I am on my own; we never had any children and I am obviously concerned about how I am going to look after myself in the future with Multiple Sclerosis.

Despite all the turmoil that is going on around me I have maintained my happiness level at 9. Recently, my happiness reached 10/10; I still have no idea how this number comes to me but each time I ask myself the question, immediately up comes a number, this time being 10. I still cannot believe that I am so peaceful and content with all that is going on around me. It is a miracle for me. I no longer fear my wife and I am full of compassion towards her. It is such a great feeling to be in a complete state of contentment and bliss. People have been so amazed with my peace and calmness given my current nightmare.

Thank you Iggy, no matter what happens from here I will always be extremely grateful for your training on the sweeping method.

Chapter 10

STOP CRAVING HAPPINESS

Let's quickly recap some of the most important points covered so far; before returning to the title of this book.

Happiness is a state of existence that most people hope, pray and wish for throughout their lives. Ironically, we often delay our happiness waiting for things, people and events to fulfil our cravings and expectation. Our aspirations don't stand still. Unfortunately, not many people actually get to a state of pure peace, contentment, joy and bliss in their lifetime. We are trapped in a never-ending cycle of suffering as we try to control and change everything around us.

The key concept of this book is that happiness is an internal state of mind, but we confuse it with external factors such as success, objects, people, image, or time and place. Happiness is in the mind and if you are happy in your mind, you are happy.

Part of achieving 10/10 happiness is that you need peace from the constant mental chatter in your mind. According to Buddhist wisdom, the main cause of chatter, turbulence and suffering in your mind is the existence of cravings and aversions. A craving exists in your mind in the form of a thought or emotion for something you want or desire. Every craving left unsatisfied means that we suffer mentally, we worry, we stress, we get frustrated and angry. Unfortunately, we all have many cravings that are left unfulfilled; some that we are even unaware of, which explains the constant mental suffering. Like cravings, we also have aversions, which are thoughts relating to fears, frustrations, worries, hates, regrets, dislikes, judgement and guilt. Like cravings, every aversion we have creates inner suffering.

Ancient philosophy on the subject believes that the cessation of cravings and aversions in the mind reduces suffering. A very simple truth that everyone understands but the biggest, fundamental challenge, is how do we reduce our cravings and aversions, particularly in the modern hectic, material world we live in?

Happiness sweeping is a very effective mind training technique that has helped participants dramatically improve their happiness. Developed over the last few years, the sweeping technique involves the process of identifying each and every craving or aversion, without judgement, in your subconscious mind and sweeping it away. Happiness sweeping is a process of acceptance without judgement, followed by letting go. Identifying (in a non-judgemental way) a craving, fear or frustration that causes unhappiness in your mind achieves the first part of acceptance. You start to not only 'accept' but also 'embrace' the nature of yourself and the world as it is. The sweeping technique will help you 'let go'. The sweeping technique has proven to bring peace, stillness and clarity to the mind.

Every thought we have about the past or future is essentially a craving or an aversion. When we recognise this we can deal with it by practicing happiness sweeping. As you sweep the cravings and aversions away, day by day, the thoughts of the past and future become less frequent; the results of sweeping will mean you will feel present, or in the now. Many of us spend our lives looking forward to what's next while failing to enjoy what's now.

Another way to support your happiness sweeping is by immediately creating positive energy if someone causes you to feel pain, frustration or anger. The quickest way to bring about positive energy is to bless your enemy, or the person causing you to feel this pain. Bless and wish them happiness, peace, joy, bliss, lots of prosperity and abundance.

The Ego self is a major barrier that prevents people from achieving a life of peace, contentment, joy and bliss. In order to tame the Ego self and nourish the Inner self, we now know we can turn the 'less Ego, more others' (LEMO) switch *on* in our minds. The practice of loving kindness and compassion is how we turn the LEMO switch *on*. Extensive research has shown that by practicing loving kindness and compassion to others, and importantly, to yourself, creates happiness in your mind.

Finally, maintaining the 'right view' is to have a view that is free of judgement. Judgement originates from cravings and aversions in the mind. Instead, having a 'neutral view' or no view, allows you to be open and accepting; enriching the flow of loving kindness and compassion.

FINAL HAPPINESS SWEEPING EXERCISE
Before we conclude, let's try one last sweeping exercise before your journey towards happiness begins!

CRAVINGS (EXAMPLES)

- *My craving to be liked is gone.*
- *My craving to be financially secure is gone.*
- *My craving to be loved and appreciated is gone.*
- *My craving to be successful is gone.*
- *My craving to .... is gone*

(Now your turn; say your personal cravings aloud)

AVERSIONS (FEAR)

- *My fear of being judged is gone.*
- *My fear of dying and leaving my loved ones is gone.*
- *My fear of getting sick is gone.*
- *My fear of not being able to support my family is gone.*
- *My fear of ....is gone.*

(carry on with your personal fears)

AVERSIONS (WORRY)

- *My worry about work situation is gone.*
- *My worry about my parents' health is gone.*
- *My worry about passing my exams is gone.*
- *My worry about .... is gone.*

(carry on with your personal worries)

AVERSIONS (FRUSTRATION)

- *My frustration of colleagues not performing their jobs properly is gone.*
- *My frustration for the bad drivers on the road is gone.*

- *My frustration for my child not completing homework is gone.*
- *My frustration of my boss is gone.*
- *My frustration of …………….. is gone.*

(carry on with your personal frustrations)

FINALLY, STOP CRAVING HAPPINESS

Dr Daryl Chow MA PhD (Psych) is a practicing psychologist who believes there is something dysfunctional about our deep cravings for the pursuit of happiness. In an online blog post entitled *The Dark Side of Pursuing Happiness* (2015), Chow describes cravings to be, *"like most things in our lives. If we eat too much of it, it spoils the good of having enough"*. He believes that his profession in mental health is guilty for propagating this overly simplistic and self-defeating idea. He continues, "sometimes it's bubble wrapped in the paddings of positive psychology".

Chow admits his surprise when he came across a recent study by Ford, Mauss, and Gruber published in a well-regarded American Psychological Association journal, *Emotion* (2015). The study addressed potential negative consequences to people who valued happiness to an extreme. It turns out that people who value happiness to an extreme tend to have worse psychological health including depression. Clearly, this group had major cravings for happiness.

Chow also quotes an experiment by Jonathan Schooler (American Psychologist and Professor of Psychological and Brain Sciences at the University of California), which provides an example of the downside to chasing happiness as a goal. Schooler asked two groups of people to do the following:

Group 1: Listen to a piece of music "in order to make yourself feel as happy as possible".

Group 2: Simply "Listen to a piece of music".

Some of them were also asked to monitor their "Happiness meter" as they listened to the music. Chow reveals the study's results:

1. Listening to music with the goal of trying to become happy **reduced** happiness; and
2. Monitoring one's happiness while listening to music also **reduced** happiness.

According to Chow, the very act of monitoring and seeking happiness has a paradoxical effect on feeling happy. *"Instead, focus on the process. By this I mean, focus on the stuff that matters to you. Take your eyes off the hedonistic desire to get the results."*

The study created cravings (goal) to be happier in Group 1. As we know, cravings create worry, dissatisfaction, mental turbulence and ultimately, unhappiness. The psychological experiment referenced by Chow is an example of the key concept in this book; cravings are the source of unhappiness. Group 2 were the happier group as they listened to music without any expectations (cravings); Group 2 was present without distraction and were able to thus enjoy the journey rather than the ultimate destination.

In Chapter 2, as you may recall I asked you the following questions:

1. Do you want to be happy?
2. Do you want your children to be happy?
3. Do you want your spouse or partner to be happy?
4. Do you want your family and friends to be happy?

The answers you gave in Chapter 2 were probably all affirmative; a resounding 'yes' to each question. A resounding YES to all four questions. Unfortunately, we have all been taught and programmed from a very young age that the pursuit of happiness is what our ultimate life goal should be. We all want to be happy and we all want everyone around us to be happy. Having now read this book, can you see that we have set ourselves up for a life-time of mental suffering?!

1. The desire to be happy is a CRAVING
2. The desire for our children to be happy is a CRAVING
3. The desire for our spouse/partner to be happy is a CRAVING
4. The desire for our family/friends to be happy is a CRAVING

These are all very deep cravings that have been instilled in all of us since we were young. Here is the problem: craving to be happy creates unhappiness. Yes, it is extremely counter-intuitive but it is the secret to happiness.

So now it is time to *sweep* the cravings for happiness away.

- *"My craving to be happy is gone."*
- *"My craving for my children to be happy is gone."*
- *"My craving for my spouse/partner to be happy is gone."*
- *"My craving for my family/friends to be happy is gone."*

The first and most important part along the journey towards happiness is to stop the craving for happiness. This is a major desire we all have had for most of our lives. Once you 'let go' of these craving, the void left behind in your mind will gradually fill with happiness.

I WANT HAPPINESS

Finally, there is a story about a young man who approached Buddha to request inner happiness. Buddha asked the man what he wanted and the man said *"I want happiness"*. Buddha replied, *"Get rid of 'I' as that is associated with Ego. Get rid of 'want' as that is associated with craving. When you get rid of 'I' and 'want' what do you have left?"*.

The greatest life paradox, the key element of manifesting what you want is actually letting go of what you want.

So, Stop Craving Happiness

Teresa's Story...

I was very worried about my father who was undergoing stage 4 prostate cancer treatment. I feared about his health degrading. The paralysing fear of losing him made me very sad and worried. When I talked to him and saw what he was going through, I felt very helpless and distressed most of the time. I then felt this stopped me from enjoying time with my kids and family. I also worried about other things like buying a family home, improving my finances and advancing my career. My happiness level fluctuated at around 6/10. Somehow, I had this thought that I didn't deserve to be happy. I certainly did not know how it would feel to be 10/10 happy.

It was about then when Iggy taught me the technique and it helped me tremendously. I am blessed and grateful to Iggy for helping me in making this happiness shift. By being able to sweep my fears, cravings and expectations of self and others, helped me make that shift. The sweeping technique resulted in creating more inner peace, acceptance and a joyful feeling. I became more aware of my inner state and I am able to catch any fear or craving early and then sweep them away immediately.

Through this regular sweeping and meditation, I feel that my happiness is now 10/10. My father is still suffering from cancer. For the first time in my life, I am feeling blissful, happy and have less worry and mental chatter. I am no longer a self-critic and this has increased my confidence and helped me to be more focused on tasks at hand. I no longer have fear about my future and now have very less expectations of myself and others that matter the most to me in my life.

HAPPINESS CHECKLIST

- ☐ *PRACTISE HAPPINESS SWEEPING DAILY*
- ☐ *SWEEP PAST AND FUTURE CRAVINGS & AVERSIONS*
- ☐ *BLESS YOUR ENEMIES*
- ☐ *LESS EGO, MORE OTHERS*
- ☐ *MAINTAIN A NON-JUDGEMENTAL VIEW*
- ☐ *PRACTISE LOVING KINDNESS & COMPASSION*
- ☐ *TRY MEDITATION*

FINAL DEDICATION

To my dear father, Joseph, who taught me to be a great teacher and leader.

At the ripe old age of 87, he has commenced learning French.

He has inspired me to believe that you are never too old to learn and grow.

Thanks Dad for everything.

THE AUTHOR

Iggy Tan BSc MBA GAICD

Iggy Tan is a successful mining and chemical industry CEO, a Rotarian and author of *Ban the Performance Appraisal* (2016). Iggy also volunteers his time as a 'happiness coach', mentoring others in the art of happiness. While psychology was not part of his tertiary education, through personal experience with depression, Iggy has garnered a deep understanding of social psychology, the human condition and mental health. Over the last few years of his personal journey, Iggy created ***Happiness Sweeping®,*** a mind training technique that has helped many people dramatically improve their personal happiness and overall sense of well-being. Iggy coined the term '10/10 happiness' meaning the ultimate state of inner peace, contentment, joy and bliss. Iggy considers himself 10/10 happy through regular happiness sweeping and meditation. Iggy now shares this technique with the world. The book's proceeds will support Rotary International and suicide prevention not-for-profit R U OK?

Iggy holds a Master of Business Administration from the University of Southern Cross, a Bachelor of Science from the University of Western Australia and is a graduate of the Australian Institute of Company Directors.